D1634196

C015528919

THE
HOME FRONT
IN
WORLD WAR TWO

THE HOME FRONT IN WORLD WAR TWO

'Keep Calm and Carry On'

SUSIE HODGE

First published in Great Britain in 2012 by
REMEMBER WHEN
an imprint of
Pen and Sword Books Ltd
47 Church Street
Barnsley
South Yorkshire S70 2AS

ISBN 978 1 84884 818 4

A CIP record for this book is available from the British Library.

Printed and bound in England by
CPI Group (UK) Ltd, Croydon, CR0 4YY

Typeset in Plantin by
CHIC GRAPHICS

Pen & Sword Books Ltd incorporates the imprints of
Pen & Sword Aviation, Pen & Sword Family History, Pen & Sword Maritime, Pen & Sword Military, Pen & Sword Discovery, Wharncliffe Local History, Wharncliffe True Crime, Wharncliffe Transport, Pen & Sword Select, Pen & Sword Military Classics, Leo Cooper, Remember When, The Praetorian Press, Seaforth Publishing and Frontline Publishing

For a complete list of Pen and Sword titles please contact
Pen and Sword Books Limited
47 Church Street, Barnsley, South Yorkshire, S70 2AS, England
E-mail: enquiries@pen-and-sword.co.uk
Website: www.pen-and-sword.co.uk

CONTENTS

INTRODUCTION

*"Let us therefore brace ourselves to our duties and so bear
ourselves that, if the British Empire and its Commonwealth last
for a thousand years, men will still say, 'This was their finest
hour.'"*Winston Churchill, 18th June 1940

On the day that World War Two was declared, 3rd September 1939,
the *Evening Chronicle* ran the headline: "Play your part with
calmness and courage." Ten months later, and one month after
Winston Churchill had become Prime Minister, he continued to urge
the British public to remain resolute and positive.

World War Two had a far greater effect on ordinary lives than
World War One had ever had and the spirit of those who experienced
it resulted in some remarkable achievements in the attempt to not
only survive, but to sustain the morale of everyone else fighting for
the same cause. This book investigates how the lives changed of some
of the 90 per cent of the British population who remained civilians
throughout World War Two; how they dealt with the difficulties and
how, through a sense of solidarity, a spirit of defiance and innovative
approaches to a wide variety of problems, they helped Britain to
emerge victorious after almost six gruelling years.

Many of these unsung heroes have been interviewed or
remembered in this book and many other primary and secondary
sources have been investigated to compile an image of how a nation
faced adversity together. From these personal perspectives, the book
paints a picture of how, through enterprise and endeavour, many

managed to improve exceptionally difficult lives by "making do and mending"; not just with fabrics and thread, but in almost every aspect of their existence; from growing food, to cooking with new ingredients, to salvaging, learning new skills, joining voluntary services or helping others directly, all of which had an impact on so many facets of life during the war.

Although being stalwart and brave at home while others fought abroad has been an aspect of conflicts for centuries, from the beginning World War Two brought unprecedented hardship to the British public. Evacuation, air raids and aerial bombardment, gas masks, ID cards, conscription, widespread shortages and rationing, blackouts, the Blitz, barrage balloons and anti-aircraft guns were just a few of the privations, horrors and worries that pervaded life in Britain that the public learned to live with. When mainland Europe fell to the Nazis in 1939, Britain was suddenly completely isolated. It had the effect of drawing the British people closer together, forging greater bonds, a firmer sense of involvement, refusal to yield and a more determined effort to defeat the enemy. Of course, there were exceptions. Some coped with the hardships in less than honest ways and long separations between couples prompted promiscuity in various quarters. There was a rise in crime and prostitution, while many suffered with psychological problems resulting from the stress. But on the whole, the entire population bolstered each other with incredible cheerfulness, courage and stamina.

Strange new world
From the moment war was declared, everyone dutifully carried their gas masks and identity cards. Streets were transformed by Air Raid Precautions (ARP) measures, including the sandbagging of buildings. In preparation for Nazi attacks, barrage balloons floated over towns, cities, industrial areas, ports and harbours while on the ground, anti-aircraft guns (known by most as "ack-ack" guns) could be heard practising regularly. Searchlight beams seeking out enemy aircraft in the sky were highly visible at night. Food was not immediately rationed, but from early on, there were shortages of butter and sugar. Petrol was rationed and some other consumer goods were also in

short supply. In the war's first days, all places of entertainment were closed for fear of bombing, while embryonic television transmissions ceased and beaches were all sealed off with barbed wire in case of invasion by the enemy, for the extent of the war.

Being the home-makers and often bringing up children, women were the instigators and architects of most of the creativity and enterprise in and around the home. With huge resolve, while retaining the "homemaking" ideal that they had held before the war, housewives took up the enormous challenges that this particular war threw at them. Many also did war work, whether paid or voluntary and their resolve and refusal to let the situation overwhelm them played a large part in helping Britain win the war. At the start of the war the majority of women did not work outside the home but by 1942 400,000 British women were serving in the army, navy and air force. Women pilots flew planes from factories to RAF bases and when young men were called into the armed forces, millions of women worked in roles that had been traditionally the realms of men; in industry, building ships, aircraft, vehicles and arms, on buses and trains, in factories, hospitals and schools. Around 80,000 women joined the Women's Land Army and worked in the fields. Others remained in their homes, caring for children, looking after elderly relatives, taking part in voluntary organisations and generally helping in the war effort and bolstering morale. Most suddenly found themselves on their own in sole charge of their households, which could include as well as their own children, evacuees, billeted workers or relatives who had been bombed out of their homes. They quickly learned how to deal with the changes and to protect those in their care. As the war continued, they learned how to make nourishing meals from fewer ingredients and they became adept at growing, mending, repairing and preparing. Collectively, they faced the harsh conditions they found themselves in with courage and creativity. As the skills and time of civilians became essential to the war effort, the role of women in particular became invaluable. Housewives were urged to "Keep the home fires burning" and they were often described by politicians and journalists as "the force behind the fighting line".

A common cause

The phrase "Home Front" became used to acknowledge the contribution by all civilians who were fighting battles 24 hours a day on a domestic level, with rationing, recycling, repairing, relief and assistance and war work. Everyone was encouraged to do as much as they could to help the common cause. Additionally, those men who were left at home for whatever reason did far more around the house than they had ever done before. In 1943, *Good Housekeeping* featured an article called "Danger – Men at Work". It began: "Through force of circumstance men are today having to do housework. They do it ponderously and reluctantly, but still they do quite a lot of it." The article continued that men who found themselves in the Forces having to wash up for hundreds, or even those who remained at home and helped out with the housework, began inventing new solutions to make life easier, such as changing the shapes of cups and plates to make washing and stacking simpler. Already, out of adversity, innovative ideas were emerging.

Doing their bit

Many civilian women served with voluntary organisations such as the Women's Auxiliary Fire Service, the Women's Auxiliary Police Corps and in the Air Raid Precautions (later Civil Defence) services. Others did voluntary welfare work with the Salvation Army and the Women's Voluntary Service for Civil Defence (WVS), which had been founded in 1938 and by the start of the war had more than 300,000 volunteers. Some women joined the Special Operations Executive (SOE), which used them in high-danger roles as secret agents and underground radio operators in Nazi-occupied Europe.

From an early age, children became involved in helping with the war effort and many were remarkably inventive and resourceful. Young children mainly helped to salvage and collect waste products for re-use, such as paper, rags, tin foil and jam jars. Older children generally helped by learning first aid, assisting the elderly to grow vegetables and to get to air raid shelters, helping in harvests, helping with home repairs, knitting items to keep soldiers warm and making much-needed splints and bandages. But of course, many children's lives were disrupted through evacuation. By 1945, approximately 3.5 million people, mainly children, had experienced evacuation.

The sense of purpose that developed over the war years has become legendary; from the smallest efforts to the largest, as human nature – on the whole – emerged triumphant. It was a time of great endurance and innovation. For example, making do and mending was not just about renovating old clothes; it was a mammoth operation undertaken by the majority of those remaining at home and included household repairs, making new items out of old, and inventing useful things out of what was available. And all this was undertaken by people who did not really know much about the progress of the war – they only had censored letters, newspaper reports and newsreels to rely on. Propaganda reached them and stories they heard or read about were not always clear or accurate. Uncertainty, insecurity and fear were suppressed by resolve and resilience.

Shortages

By early 1941 when merchant ships were being sunk at a rate of three a day, shortages were at their worst. The small amount of meat and sugar that each person in Britain was allowed was not easy to obtain, butter was reduced to two ounces a week per person, with one ounce of cheese and two ounces of tea. In 1942, Winston Churchill declared that "Tea is more important than ammunition" and advised that servicemen had as many cups as they wanted and that for them tea would be issued without restriction. But as the war continued with no sign of a breakthrough, the rationing at home had to be confronted with increased determination and imagination.

Soon, shortages occurred in almost everything and the most unlikely items acquired rarity value. As a result, National Salvage Drives became an important feature, organised and collected by individuals from the WVS. With the threat of sudden death or maiming both at the Front and at home, an underlying sense of purpose emerged as a united feeling among the British. Overall, it is arguable that if the proud and determined battle by British civilians faced with such sacrifice and personal cost had not been fought so resolutely, the ultimate victory might not have been achieved.

I am so grateful to the many people who have shared their stories with me, who made a vital and creative contribution to our history without even realising it. Their personal memories and indomitable spirits are an inspiration to us all.

1

THE HOME FRONT

"There may be dark days ahead, and war can no longer be confined to the battlefield, but we can only do the right as we see the right..." King George VI, 3rd September 1939

Preparing for war

At least a year before it actually started, Britain began preparing for war. After World War One, there was an underlying sense of fear in many countries as the ideologies of Communism, Socialism and Fascism prompted violent reactions in unexpected quarters. In 1932 Shanghai was bombed by Japan and in 1937, in the Spanish Civil War, the Basque town of Guernica was bombed by Hitler's Luftwaffe. Within a year, the British government started building new warships and increasing its arms, but it realised that another war, following on so soon from the 1914-18 Great War and the Depression of the early 1930s, would not just involve soldiers; it would disrupt and threaten the lives of civilians in Britain more than any other previous conflict. So along with building weapons and warships, the government began taking precautions against anticipated dangers and difficulties that might be faced at home.

"Sleep quietly in your beds"

Planning for an integrated home defence was intensified and information leaflets began being produced on practically every aspect of living. The first of these leaflets to be distributed to every British household had been drawn up in 1937. On 30th September 1938, the prime minister Neville Chamberlain returned from Germany, waving a document and declaring to waiting crowds: "This bears Herr Hitler's name and mine, vowing that our two countries will never again go to war against each other." That night, from a window of 10 Downing Street, he addressed more joyous crowds: "I believe it is peace for our time. Go home and sleep quietly in your beds." Less than a year later, after continued aggression by Hitler and his forces invaded Poland, a disconsolate Chamberlain broadcast from the Cabinet Room that Hitler had defaulted on his part of the agreement and consequently, Britain was at war with Germany.

In July 1939, every household in Britain had received four official Civil Defence pamphlets. Pamphlet number one was called *Some Things You Should Know If War Should Come*. While trying not to alarm readers, it outlined the main schemes being prepared by the authorities and explained that 'it is everyone's duty to be prepared for the possibility of war.' The almost constant supply of information from the authorities to the public continued throughout the war, motivating, encouraging, informing, controlling and overwhelmingly trying to protect citizens and win the war. At this time most people, although realising that war was probable, did not know what to expect. They did not then know that Hitler would try to beat them into submission; that the demands on those living through it at home would be massive, leaving them exhausted and impoverished, but that they would rise to the occasion and develop a resilience and optimism that would become legendary.

The British public at that time were more deferential and compliant than they are today. They followed the government's advice and recommendations dutifully and unquestioningly, believing it was in the national interest to do so. From the moment war was declared, advice came pouring in from all quarters, from booklets and leaflets to magazine and newspaper articles, as well as posters, films (at the cinema) and messages on the radio (wireless). Posters showed how to put on a gas mask, how to plant vegetables, and how to collect scrap metal and they declared "coughs and sneezes spread diseases, catch your germs in your handkerchiefs", "careless words cost lives" and "Be like Dad, keep Mum". Recipes for using powdered egg, powdered potato and dried apple rings abounded and posters, radio, films and newspapers were used to keep up people's spirits, to make the most of victories and to make fun of the enemy. This government propaganda was vital throughout the war as a means of communication and of boosting morale – and the people welcomed it – but being individuals, they also used their own ingenuity wherever they could. It was very much a period of encouraging people to help themselves and others and the abundance of information and advice was generally welcomed as support during a time of genuine fear and uncertainty.

Austerity begins

Before war was declared, the government encouraged all to plant vegetables on any spare land they may have to supplement the rationing that would almost certainly occur. The many pamphlets sent to households contained information on what to do in situations such as air raids or gas attacks, as well as on how to make rations stretch further and how to keep healthy. As a safety measure, from the moment war was declared, cinemas, dance halls and other places of entertainment were closed, but after widespread objections it was realised that the nation needed entertainment to sustain its spirits and within a week most had re-opened.

One of the many early and unexpected consequences of shortages was the shrinking of newspapers. As paper rationing came into force, most newspapers diminished and for the duration of the war, the majority struggled to include more than eight pages. *The Times* maintained eight to 10 pages for a while; *The Daily Express* had between 10 to 24 pages until mid-1940, while *The Star, The Evening Standard* and the *Daily Mirror* kept to eight pages for most of the war. Naturally, all newspapers were crammed full of reports on the war's progression, usually as much uplifting news as possible and also squeezed in were football and cricket bulletins and film and theatre reviews. Wasting no space, newspapers were invaluable as one of the primary means through which people at home found out what was happening in the war.

Petrol was rationed from September 1939. Initially, a small allowance was permitted for domestic vehicles, but this stopped by the summer of 1942. It soon became apparent that driving was not practical and most personal vehicles were put out of action "for the duration"; a phrase that became commonly used to describe the extent of the war. Petrol rationing initially provoked complaints, although the overwhelming attitude among the British throughout the period was stoical; that the war had to be won whatever it took. Even if drivers had enough petrol however, the dangers of driving in the blackout led to a 20mph speed limit being introduced after dark. Train travel was not restricted, but people were asked to consider each journey. Posters queried "Is your journey really necessary?" Taking fewer journeys was partly to conserve fuel and partly to leave room for travelling servicemen and women. Inevitably, there was a surge in the use of buses, resulting in queues and overcrowding. Most people travelling short distances walked or cycled, but the companies who made pushbikes were now producing aircraft parts and weapons, so bicycles became highly sought after. Due to the shortage of natural latex, scientists collaborated and synthetic Butyl rubber was invented to create inner tubes. This was one example of enterprise that was triggered by the war that changed the lives of many throughout the world – both then and into the twenty-first century.

Masks, balloons and cards

Fearing that poison gas bombs would be dropped by the German Luftwaffe over Britain, the British government decided to issue gas masks to everyone. The second leaflet that households had received in July 1939 dealt with gas masks – how to store them and how to put them on. By 1940, 38 million gas masks in cardboard boxes had been distributed across Britain. Adult masks were black while children had "Mickey Mouse" masks with red rubber pieces and bright eye rims. Babies were put inside large containers that mothers had to pump full of air. Jean Pink remembered:

> "When war broke out, I was five years old and living in Edgware in North London. As soon as war started, my mum, my auntie and I pushed my cousin in his pram to a church hall to collect our gas masks. I was given a Mickey Mouse mask but it was so scary, I screamed! So they gave me a black one like

my mum's and auntie's, which was still terrifying. Everyone looked menacing in them. They had bits that jutted-out with holes in and a rubber hood to stretch over your face, secured at the back with a thick rubber strap. When you put your mask on, it was hot inside and difficult to breathe. The strong smell of the rubber made me feel sick. Just as frightening was the 'mask' they covered my little cousin Michael's whole pram with. Michael didn't like it, which made us both cry. Every time I left the house, my mum or auntie would say 'Have you got your gas mask?' We weren't allowed anywhere without them in their bulky cardboard boxes. Cinemas wouldn't allow us in without them and we even had to carry them if we were playing in the street.

At about the same time, a field nearby was filled with barrage balloons which were sent up into the sky to deter any German pilots trying to fly over London. In the sky, the barrage balloons looked small and harmless, but on the ground, they were enormous and terrifying."

With the fear of poison gas bombs, the government recruited chemists as local Gas Identification Squads. Between them they wrote a "Chart of War Gases", which was distributed throughout Britain. To help the public identify the various types of poisons that might be dropped, the chart listed tear gases, choking gases, blister gases, nose irritant gases and systematic poisoning gas, with information about first aid and treatment for each. The tops of post boxes were painted with yellowish-green gas detector paint that would change colour if there was a gas attack. A popular book was published: *ARP – A Practical Guide for the Householder and Air Raid Warden* containing a section called "Hints for householders to prepare for an emergency".

Since 1938, the government had introduced a system of air raid warnings, which was practised so that everyone was sure of what they had to do when they heard them. To warn people that there was gas about, after the usual siren warning of imminent bombings, Air Raid Wardens would sound the gas rattle and then everyone would know to put on their gas masks. The gas "all-clear" was the ringing of hand bells. Not carrying gas masks was a punishable offence, but a survey in November 1940 suggested that only about seventy-five per cent of people in London were obeying this rule. Air Raid Wardens were instructed to carry out monthly inspections of gas masks and to fine anyone caught without a mask. If a person lost theirs they had to pay for its replacement.

Barrage balloons

In the skies overhead, massive, whale-like silver-grey barrage balloons became a common sight. These enormous objects obscured important sites from the sky and forced the German pilots to fly higher, so their bombing would be less accurate. Each barrage balloon was three times the size of a cricket pitch, filled half with hydrogen and half with natural air and anchored by steel cables fixed to stationary lorries. Amid the sights of these huge floating balloons were the deafening sounds of anti-aircraft, or "ack-ack" guns.

Identity cards

By the end of September 1939, every person in Britain had been issued with an identity card; green for adults and brown for children under 16. Mainly because of fears of invasion by German spies, ID cards had to be carried by everyone and shown at checkpoints. Later, the cards were used as proof of identity for ration books. Because they had become so valuable, there were many forgeries and thefts of ID cards.

Saucepans for spitfires

On his appointment as Minister of Supply in 1940, Lord Beaverbrook began by establishing concealed munitions factories in disused mines and went on to launch a press campaign, asking the public to donate aluminium pots and pans to make fighter aircraft. "Give us your spare pots and pans and we will turn them into Spitfires and Hurricanes, Blenheims and Wellingtons" ran the headline. In response, the public donated over 70,000 tons of aluminium. In 1941 the government passed an order requisitioning all post-1850 iron gates and railings for the war effort, with a few exceptions made for items of particular historic interest.

Contemporary observers reported council workmen cutting down gates and railings, leaving only stumps behind. Yet a mystery surrounds the activity as there are fewer eyewitness reports of all the metal reaching factories. It is not certain whether all or any of it was actually used as intended. It is now believed by many that most of the metal collected (over one million tons of iron by September 1944) was not able to be used for the purpose and was scrapped. Yet the government continued the collection as it helped to boost morale; people felt that they were assisting the fight against Hitler and helping to win the war.

Blackout

On 1st September 1939, two days before the outbreak of war and following a trial run in July of that year, the whole of Britain was blacked out. Every evening between the hours of sunset and sunrise, everyone covered their windows and other openings, so that not a glimmer of light was visible from outside. Black or blue light bulbs were available, which gave off a subdued light and ARP wardens patrolled the streets to make sure that not even a speck of light could be seen. ARP wardens had the authority to report families who allowed light to show, which could lead to a heavy fine or a court appearance. *Public Information Leaflet No. 2* that had been delivered to every household that July included instructions on how to put on gas masks, how to store them and how to black out homes effectively, listing suitable fabrics for blackout curtains and blinds. These included glazed Holland, Lancaster or Italian cloth; all densely woven fabrics. Although there were no grants or subsidies for blacking out, the government tried to ensure that there was enough blackout material available in the shops. In most cases people bought plain black cotton as it was readily available and cheap (usually around two shillings a yard). But haberdashers did run short and people had to dye lighter coloured materials, following a recipe given in newspapers and magazines or making up their own. The trouble with the cheapest cotton was that it was fairly thin so it needed to be folded into two or three thicknesses before it obliterated the light completely. People were advised to test material by holding a piece against an electric light bulb. If no light showed through or only scattered pinholes of light could be seen, then the fabric was dense enough for use in the blackout. If not, another recipe was available for treating fabrics that were not opaque enough. Using a similar method and ingredients as dyeing, this involved mixing size (fabric stiffener), lamp black powder and boiling water and soaking the material in the mixture for about an hour, then wringing it out and hanging it up to dry. This was just one way that householders used their ingenuity to create effective blackouts. Some made internal shutters out of card, securing it round each window frame with battens, so sealing in the light, but also shutting out fresh air. Others used heavy calico nailed to strong wooden frames for a similar effect. Many people attached more brightly coloured and patterned fabrics to the insides of their blackout screens and some sewed on white or silver cut-out star and moon shapes to make their homes less gloomy. Daphne Roberts, a child living in Plaistow recollects:

"I remember having black curtains between the window and our usual, coloured curtains and how we covered the windows with sticky tape in case they shattered in the blasts. Some people put boards up at their windows. It felt quite airless."

If they were not able to afford fabric, some people simply painted the insides of their windows and skylights black or navy, rendering their homes dark at all times, which did not do a lot for morale. Jean Pink recalled her childhood in London:

"Every evening as the light faded, we had to rush around our house, pulling curtains tightly so that no chink of light showed in the street. We had made blackout curtains for the windows, but over the road at my friend's house, they painted their little bathroom window black and used painted card at some other windows. We also had to criss-cross our windows with sticky tape to prevent flying splinters of glass if a bomb came close. If any light showed from the outside, you'd get a knock on the door from an ARP warden who would call out: 'Put that light out!' It was a criminal offence to show any light and you could be fined."

Shop signs and reception areas of public buildings were unlit. Low-density street lighting was allowed in some parts of Britain, but no lighting at all was allowed within 12 miles of the south-east coast. Vehicles were fitted with visors; horizontal slits across the headlights that meant they could only illuminate the road a short way ahead. Traffic lights were also fitted with slotted covers to deflect the light downwardly. At first, people were worried even to strike a match and pedestrians were urged to "wear something white at night" so they would be seen by drivers. White lines were painted along the middle of some roads, on kerb edges, around trees and lamp-posts and on car bumpers in an attempt to make it a little easier to see and be seen.

The lighting on buses was dimmed and small, low-density blue-painted light bulbs were fitted in railway carriages while blinds were pulled down after dusk, so passengers travelled in semi-darkness. Trains and buses had netting pasted on to the windows as a precaution against the dangers of shattering glass. There were no lights on railway stations and although platform edges were painted white, there were many accidents and it became fairly common for passengers to get off at the wrong station – or even to get off the train where there was no station at all. Despite the best efforts of the government to be helpful, it was said that more people died from traffic accidents in the blackout than from Nazi bombs.

Evacuation

When it became apparent to many that war was imminent, with Hitler's continued aggression and particularly after the breaking of the Munich Agreement on 15th March 1939, the British government agreed on mass evacuation. As early as 1938, it was planned that children, mothers of small children, pregnant women, invalids and the elderly would be sent from major cities to safer locations. *Public Information Leaflet No. 3* was sent to every household in July 1939. It gave details of the government's scheme for mass evacuation and on 31st August 1939 at 11.07am, the day before Hitler invaded Poland, the message to "evacuate forthwith" was issued by the government across Britain. Evacuation began the following day, on Friday, 1st September 1939 – two days before the declaration of war. Called

"Operation Pied Piper", within three days, by 4th September, 1.9 million children and other vulnerable people had been evacuated from cities to smaller towns and villages in the countryside. Stan Bell was sent to Upwell in Norfolk with his entire school; Upton House in Hackney.

"On 1st September 1939, everyone in my school assembled with our suitcases and gas masks in the playground, where we were counted. Our parents waited outside the gates. Then we were taken away on coaches by our teachers to catch a train. We had all been given paper labels, which we had to attach to our clothes, displaying our names. We had no idea where we were going, how long we'd be away or when we'd see our parents again. I found out later that the government had provided parents with a list of items to pack and I remember having in my suitcase a toothbrush, towel, underwear, pyjamas and a change of clothing. Most of the children in my school were quite poor and did not own all the listed items, such as boots, a pullover and an overcoat or mackintosh. The train journey seemed a great adventure to us. When we arrived, we were all led into a school hall. Lots of the ladies of the village came to choose children. They all picked the smallest children and soon the hall had emptied, leaving just one other boy and me – we were the tallest, so nobody wanted us – they thought we would eat too much."

This picking and choosing later became known as "the Slave Auction" as in most areas of evacuation, children were left that nobody wanted. The government paid an allowance to those who opened their homes to evacuees, but it was not much: ten shillings and six pence for one child, with another eight shillings and six pence for a second child, or for a mother and child, five shillings for the mother and three shillings for a child, which barely covered the evacuees' keep.

When there were no big bombing raids on Britain during the first few months of war, the public began calling it the "Phoney War" and by January 1940, most evacuees had returned to their homes. People stopped carrying gas masks and, although action was occurring out to sea, many civilians thought that the war would never actually happen. Then suddenly, on 9th April 1940, Nazi forces attacked Denmark and Norway. British attempts to help failed and, in May 1940, Neville Chamberlain resigned and Winston Churchill became prime minister. In his inaugural speech to the British people, Churchill said: "I have nothing to offer you but blood, toil, tears and sweat...You ask, what is our aim? I can answer in one word: victory; victory at all costs, victory in spite of all terror, victory, however long and hard the road may be; for without victory, there is no survival... Come then, let us go forward together with our united strength." Churchill's inspirational and patriotic urgings did much to uplift and encourage the British public for the next five years.

In June 1940, France fell to Germany and by the end of August 1940; Britain faced the Blitz, with the German air force firstly bombing Birmingham and Liverpool. On 7th September, the bombardment intensified when around 950 German aircraft attacked London during the day, followed by 76 consecutive nights of bombing. The initial daylight raid caused approximately 300 civilian deaths and a further 1,300 serious injuries. As the London raids stopped on 14th November, Coventry was assaulted. Other cities were also bombed as part of the Blitz, including Plymouth, Manchester and Glasgow. In July 1940 another major evacuation took place and within a few weeks 213,000 children left Britain's large industrial cities for safer locations. The government also set up a Children's Overseas Reception Board (CORB), which arranged for children to be sent to the USA, Canada and Australia. However, after the steam passenger ship the *City of Benares* was sunk by a German torpedo on 17th September killing 73 children, the programme was stopped.

Unlike the well-organised and planned evacuation programme of September 1939, this second phase was more improvised. Rather than being evacuated in large groups, such as entire schools, individuals made their own arrangements, helped by the government with the "Assisted Private Evacuation Scheme". This involved financial support for travel and accommodation for those who made their own arrangements. This phase of evacuation lasted until the end of 1941, but many who moved, stayed away until the end of the war.

Meanwhile, although the government urged the public to move children and other vulnerable people to safer areas, it always stressed that evacuation was voluntary; many chose to stay at home and take their chances rather than break up their families. In the first phase, of the five and a half million who qualified, only about a third actually went. Long after the war, Kitty Pink, who lived in London with her daughter, sister and nephew, maintained that: "If we were going to die, we decided we would all die together."

Shelters
Despite Chamberlain's optimism in September 1938, preparations for civilian protection in the event of war had continued unabated. In November 1938, two months after he had made his ill-fated agreement with Hitler, the prime minister gave Sir John Anderson, then Lord Privy Seal, responsibility for preparing air raid precautions. Numerous services were set up and local authorities began digging trenches in public parks and gardens. By the time war was declared, an estimated 500,000 people could be accommodated in the communal shelters that had been built in concrete over the trenches. Made to hold up to 50 people each, they ultimately proved to be uncomfortable, damp and smelly and they frequently flooded. Anderson also commissioned an engineer, William Patterson, to design a small, cheap shelter that could be erected in people's gardens.

In February 1939, with the prospect of war seeming inevitable, the first of these sectional steel shelters were delivered across Britain to be constructed in gardens by householders. Each shelter consisted of curved and straight panels of corrugated iron, which had to be bolted together at the top, with steel plates at each end. The most common Anderson shelter (as they became called) measured 1.95 x 1.35 metres (6½ x 4½ feet) and was buried 1.2 metres (4 feet) in the soil; it could accommodate up to six people. There was also a slightly smaller version. Barbara Matthews recalls:

"Digging a huge, deep hole…in a grassy meadow [or garden] which had never been dug up before was very hard work and the men did it with picks and shovels and no mechanical help."

Earth was heaped on the roof. In some instances, householders planted the tops of these shelters with flowers and vegetables and competitions were held in some neighbourhoods for the best-planted shelter. Some people made rockeries around their Anderson shelters and many used the dense earth packed around them for growing marrows.

The 1938 government booklet *The Protection of your Home against Air Raids* featured a list of useful items to take into a shelter: "…begin collecting those things you haven't got, one by one. Put them in a box, or in a drawer…candles and matches, hammer and nails, scissors, old newspaper and brown paper, some clean rags, needles, cotton and thread. A candle lamp or and electric hand lamp…a few tins or jars with air-tight lids for storing food, a bottle of disinfectant and a box of first aid supplies." Further lists of items included plenty of water, tinned food with a tin opener, a chest to protect food from gas contamination, soap, towels, chamber pots and toilet paper, a screen for privacy, toys, sand, pick axe and shovel and so on. The internal fitting out of shelters was left to individuals, and despite their dismal function and fundamental, unsophisticated style, individual characteristics prevailed and most people made efforts to modify theirs and make them more appealing inside. Some people built fitted bunks; others made hammocks out of old tennis nets. Twelve year old Stan Bell, who lived near Clapton Common in London, made bunk beds for his family's Anderson shelter:

"With wood from a local wood yard, I built four bunk beds to fit inside our shelter. First I made a framework and then I put slats across. My parents, grandmother and I used the shelter and we made it as comfortable as possible with mattresses and cushions on the bunks. We lit the shelter with hurricane lamps and to this day I can remember the smell of paraffin and am transported back to the shelter. We took books with us, but the noise of the bombs and ack-ack guns on the Common nearby was very loud and traumatic. It was difficult to concentrate or relax."

One month after war broke out, Anderson shelters went on sale. Any householder (with a garden) earning less than £250 a year received theirs free, while those on higher incomes (more than £5 a week) could buy one for between £7 and £10, depending on the size. By the end of the war, there were 3.6 million Anderson shelters in Britain. But because they had to be partially submerged in the ground, they were susceptible to flooding and were usually damp, draughty, noisy and cramped. Sleeping in them was difficult, as Margaret Ronaldson, living in Bow, recalled:

"When the Blitz started, we spent every night in our Anderson shelter, but it was hard to sleep as the noise of falling bombs was terrible and the ground shook violently. Mum and I used to plug our ears with cotton wool and we put lots of cushions and blankets inside the shelter to try to muffle the dreadful din."

Sheila Dunne was nine years old when war broke out and living in West London. She remembered her time in the family air raid shelter:

"At first, it was quite a novelty. We had a camping stove and we heated water to make tea. We also took the radio in there with us and listened to it as we drank tea, played cards, read and chatted. But after a few nights, we just tried to sleep in there. It was always dark and damp and very noisy."

Maisie Walker remembered:

"It was a nightly ritual to get the flask of tea, blankets, candle and sandwiches ready to take down the Anderson shelter which incidentally was always swimming in six inches of water. We could tell by the sound of the engines of the planes whether they were friend or foe. Blue [the cat] always gave us warning at least ten minutes before the siren went by clawing at the door or what was left of it. We knew that we had time to grab everything to make our way down to the shelter. It was a living nightmare to go through the continual bombing night after night…When we emerged each morning still alive it was a miracle. It was better still if we could have a cup of tea and a wash to take the grime out of our eyes from continual dust and smoke of the fires and buildings that had collapsed."

Mirrie Hull, a child in growing up in Charlton during the war, said that she, her sisters and her mother always went to bed in their pyjamas, but with their coats hanging at the end. As soon as the air raid siren sounded, she and her sisters grabbed their coats and ran down to the Anderson shelter in the garden. Anderson shelters were dark and damp, soggy at best and tended to flood at worst. Sleeping in them was difficult as they did not keep out the sound of the bombings. There were no toilet facilities, except perhaps for a bucket in the corner and people became reluctant to use them.

Those who lived through this time recall the fear, panic and disconcerting atmosphere of the blackouts and ensuing bombing raids. Although advice was forthcoming from government sources, once the bombing raids started, families and individuals were on their own and no one knew what would happen next. Stories of parents grabbing sleeping children from their beds, of disorientated elderly people being unsure of where to go and babies crying in fright are recounted by many who lived through it. By 1941, after the experiences of the Blitz, a new booklet was circulated, entitled *Air Raids – What You Must KNOW, What You Must DO*. A large section of it dealt with the problems of Anderson shelters, particularly how to counteract the damp and flooding problems. Suggestions included building runnels to draw away surface water or sealing the joints between the iron sheets with strips of rag, Hessian or rope that had been soaked with heavy oil or tar. Condensation could be lessened by painting the interiors with paint or shellac varnish and throwing sawdust on to this while the paint was wet. Or the inside of the shelter could be lined with lino, plasterboard, felt or even wallpaper could be applied to the plasterboard.

None of these methods was particularly successful however and Anderson shelters were unpopular. In addition, not everyone living in cities where most raids occurred had the necessary outdoor space. By early 1941 the Morrison shelter, named after the Minister for Home Security Herbert Morrison and designed by Lord John

Fleetwood Baker, was developed for protection inside the home. As with Anderson shelters, Morrison shelters were available free to those on low incomes (households earning less than £350 a year), while those earning more had to pay £7. Arriving in kit form, each Morrison shelter had a solid steel top plate, welded wire mesh sides, a metal base and a mattress floor. They were all two metres (6½ft) long and just over one metre wide and high (4ft), so no one could stand up in them. The sides could be taken off during the day so the shelter could be used as a table. Approximately 600,000 Morrison shelters were distributed throughout the war. Newspapers and magazines often contained features suggesting ways of passing the time in shelters during air raids and listed useful items to take in, such as eau de cologne or smelling salts, candles, matches and food. Many people packed secure bags with the family's ration books, identity cards, gas masks, insurance policies, books, games, magazines and comics and took them into the shelter during air raids.

A safe place
In 1940, the Ministry of Home Security issued a pamphlet *Your Home as an Air Raid Shelter*. Reaching homes before serious aerial raids began, the booklet gave information on erecting sectional shelters in the garden and on how to make your home as bomb-proof as possible. The idea of staying in the home rather than going out to a cold, damp and often flooded shelter outdoors was extremely appealing and a description of how to make a "Refuge Room" took up a large part of the pamphlet. A refuge room was described as being a room preferably on the ground floor or in a basement, with as few windows or doors as possible. Predominantly intended to protect families in the event of poison gas attacks, few people actually created refuge rooms as the pamphlet gave instructions for householders to adapt the room themselves and few had the time, space or inclination to create such a room. The cupboard under the stairs was another good option, or cellars that could be reinforced with steel. The pamphlet suggested that anyone living in upstairs flats should come to an arrangement with neighbours downstairs.

Under the heading "Protection of Glass in Windows" the pamphlet explained: "You should realise that nothing you can stick on to glass will prevent it being broken, nor will even increase its chance of remaining unbroken when a bomb explodes nearby. But a good covering, properly stuck on, will prevent glass flying in small dangerous pieces and may even hold a badly cracked and bulged pane in place enough to keep out the weather for a time. Coverings of this kind are suitable where curtains and blinds are used for blackout." Following this was a detailed list of various materials that could be used to protect windows, including paper or cardboard, transparent wrapping films and cellulose acetate film. Whatever material was used however, it soon became brittle and had to be replaced every two to three months. Other options included hanging blankets over doorways and windows, using sandbags or boxes of earth to buffer windows and criss-crossing glass panes with strips of gummed tape. In the 1930s, lead strip had been popular for creating leaded light latticed windows. By 1940, it was renamed ARP Protection for Windows and was used to secure windows from possible blasts; one of many examples of business using their initiative to survive and to provide an essential service during the war.

Safety underground
Before the war, government ministers had discussed the possibility of civilians using tube stations and other underground tunnels in London in the event of bombing raids. Several ministers were against this because they believed that such places with their lack of toilet facilities would be unhealthy, plus there was a real risk of people falling on to the lines, or a further concern that people would not leave the stations once the raid was over. When the intensive bombing of London began on 7th September 1940, there was a call by many to change the policy, but the government refused. Then, after incessant bombardment on the night of 19th September, thousands of Londoners flocked en masse into the relative safety of Underground stations. Many arrived in the afternoon, in advance of the air raid warning, equipped with bedding and food for the night. Commuting and the rush hour continued around them, but the police did not interfere and some station managers even took the initiative to provide additional toilet facilities. The government had no option but to capitulate and on 21st September, it formally allowed the

public to use Underground stations as air raid shelters, fitting out 79 stations with bunks for 22,000 people, first aid facilities and chemical toilets. Within a short time, 124 canteens had opened in various parts of the Underground system to provide those sheltering with comforting sustenance and to take their minds off what was happening above. Salvation Army officers, who helped with emergency services during the war, also often handed out sweets to children sheltering in the Underground with their families. Although not rationed until 1942, sweets were already becoming difficult to obtain, so this kind act helped to take children's minds off their fears. Air raid wardens were also appointed in the Underground stations, to supervise, to administer first aid and assist in the event of flooding.

In Chislehurst, Kent, there are man-made chalk and flint mines that are known as caves. In September 1940, when the aerial bombardment of London began, the caves were used as an air raid shelter. Special trains were put on from London every night to Chislehurst so that people could sleep in the caves and soon it became an underground city of approximately 15,000 inhabitants, with electric lighting, a chapel and a hospital. Music concerts and church services were held there. People camped with mattresses and candles; makeshift toilets were set up behind canvas and because they could still hear the bombs, but muffled and in the distance, they felt relatively safe. Another popular place during air raids was "Tilbury Arches" in Stepney, London. The local council turned this into a large public shelter for 3,000 people, but on some nights over 16,000 people squeezed in.

Along with the mood of acceptance and endurance, many people became fatalistic about sheltering and, tired of the nightly bombings, remained in their beds. Others did the opposite and slept in shelters whether or not there was an air raid. In November 1940, the government did a survey of people in Central London to find out who was sheltering where. The results proved that four per cent were sheltering in the Underground system; nine per cent were sheltering in public shelters and 27 per cent were sheltering in Anderson or Morrison shelters at home, while the rest either did not shelter at all, or went under the stairs, in basements or refuge rooms during air raids.

Fire-fighting

In August 1939, a fifth booklet was issued by the government. Entitled *Fire Precautions in Wartime*, it was mainly about incendiary bombs and methods of tackling them. Incendiary bombs were fairly small and hundreds were dropped at a time. On impact they ignited and burned, so everyone was urged to be prepared. The booklet instructed: "...In Civil Defence, EVERYBODY has a part to play. This is especially true of fire-fighting. In every house there should be one or more people ready to tackle a fire bomb." Explaining that most bombs would hit and set fire to roofs, attics and upstairs rooms, the pamphlet gave instructions about clearing out lofts and dealing with these fires. Simply throwing water from a bucket would aggravate the flames as the main combustible component of most incendiary bombs was white phosphorus. The recommended method of extinguishing the fires from incendiaries was to use a hand-operated stirrup pump developed for the purpose and then to smother the bomb in dry sand from a bucket. From the start of the Blitz, firemen worked constantly, not only putting out fires but also tackling explosions and the aftermath. Bombs in warehouses were especially dangerous due to many of the products stored in them, for example, highly flammable alcohol and paint. Groups of neighbours organised rotas, volunteering as fire watchers to take some of the workload from the fire service and to contend with small local fires. Each group was issued with a bucket for sand, a bucket for water and a stirrup pump and each was taught by the fire brigade to use stirrup pumps properly. Some groups of neighbours bought their own stirrup pumps to be shared by the whole street. In September 1940, a law was passed, requiring factories and businesses to appoint employees to watch for incendiary bombs outside working hours.

Blackouts, bombs and shortages were just a few of the burdens on individuals. But an attitude of unshakable fortitude in the face of adversity emerged, becoming known as the Blitz, Dunkirk or wartime spirit. Collectively and individually, people determined to keep up their own and their family's morale by whatever means possible. Generosity of spirit came to the fore in most (although theft, looting and prostitution also rose, particularly during the blackouts) and many turned to vital war work or voluntary services.

2
WOMEN AT WAR

"Today we are calling all women. Every woman in the country is needed to pull her weight to the utmost...We are fighting for our lives, for our freedom and our future." Diana Thomas, broadcasting on the BBC *Home Service* in May 1941

When this radio appeal was made, there was an acute shortage of workers in Britain. Since October 1939 all men between the ages of 18 and 41, not working in the 'reserved occupations' of miners, farmers, scientists, merchant seamen and dock, railway and utility workers, were conscripted. Women were not called up as it was believed that taking mothers and wives away from their families would damage the balance of domestic life. Most thought a woman's place should be in the home. But by the spring of 1940, the British government realised that at least one and half million more workers were desperately needed and the only way this could be achieved was by recruiting women. As Diana Thomas continued in her broadcast:

"...We are all in it together, and what is already being done by other women, you can do. Don't be afraid of being alone in your sacrifice – however great it may be... All those little things that are so important in every woman's life – we treasure them and cling to them, they are our life-blood. And now we have got to fight for them. Isn't it worth it?"

Government schemes also encouraged women to volunteer and although many did, many more were needed. From early in 1941, every woman in Britain aged 18 to 60 had to be registered with the Ministry of Labour for war work; but they were not conscripted. By the middle of that year however, the British government made a bold move and decided to conscript women, considering this to be the only way to move forward and to stand a chance of winning the war. In December 1941, the National Service Act made the conscription of women legal in Britain. At first, only single women between the ages of 20 to 30 were called up and were allowed to opt for enrolment either into the armed forces or into industry. By mid-1943, almost 90 per cent of single women and 80 per cent of married women were employed in essential work for the war effort. On 3rd December 1941, *The Daily Telegraph* reported: 'Unmarried Women to be Conscripted'. The column began:

> "Nearly 1,700,000 unmarried women between 20 and 30, and 70,000 youths between 18½ and 19, are among the vast number of people affected by the Government's new conscription plans, which were announced by Mr Churchill in the House of Commons yesterday."

The article went on to explain the new parliamentary act; outlining who would now be liable for national service and giving the main points made by Winston Churchill in his speech on the subject. It listed the organisations for which the unmarried female recruits might be called. In the same speech, Churchill had declared that men from 41 to 50 were now also to be called up. Even the number of Conscientious Objectors dropped drastically at this point and the whole shape of people's lives changed entirely once more.

Signing up
All three military services were open for women to join – the army, the air force and the navy. Women were also appointed as air raid wardens. In 1943, Rosalie Somers, aged 18, was working as an air raid warden in Hammersmith, London:

"The most traumatic part of my job was digging and searching for survivors after a bomb had blown up part of a street. The devastation was dreadful – the smell; the homes ripped apart; the mess; but worst of all, to try to find people alive, who hadn't been blasted to smithereens or suffocated under the rubble. When we searched a bomb site, we did it in silence to try to hear anything, like tapping or muffled noises, in case someone might be still alive under there. Whatever happened, you had to keep cheerful and hopeful – everyone did."

Apart from actually fighting, women in the Armed forces did the same work as men, but they were mainly given "safer" jobs. Women in the Forces received two-thirds of the pay of their male counterparts. The Women's Royal Naval Service (WRNS) was originally formed in 1916 during World War One and was the first of the armed forces to recruit women. It was re-formed for World War Two in the spring of 1939. All eligible women living near naval ports could apply to join. WRNS did not go to sea on fighting warships, but took over male roles as cooks, clerks, code experts and electricians; so that more men were free to fight. In the army, women joined the Auxiliary Territorial Service (ATS), which was formed in 1938. To attract female applicants, the recruiting posters were intentionally glamorous, but on joining, women were employed in rather mundane occupations, such as drivers, cleaners, cooks, translators or administrators. Many worked in the Anti-Aircraft Command, tracking and aiming ack-ack guns on enemy planes over Britain, but only men were allowed to actually fire the guns. Later in the war, women in the ATS were also employed as welders, carpenters, armourers, draughtsmen and electricians; all specialist, previously entirely male occupations. By July 1942, there were 217,000 women in the ATS.

The Women's Royal Air Force (WRAF) originally closely followed the formation of the men's Royal Air Force (RAF) in April 1918, but it was disbanded in 1920. In the summer of 1939, the Women's Auxiliary Air Force (WAAF) was re-formed. As previously, it came under the administration of the RAF and initially, like the other services, WAAFs were recruited to work as clerks, kitchen orderlies and drivers, so that the men could be released for front-line duties. As the war continued, women were given more responsibilities, such as working in radar stations, tracking enemy bombers, analysing and intercepting codes, or maintaining and flying barrage balloons. At first, it was believed that women would not have the strength to operate the massive barrage balloons, but they turned out to be surprisingly good at it and eventually, women ran more than 1,000 barrage balloon sites throughout Britain. By the end of the war, 70 per cent of the WAAF worked in skilled roles, such as engineering and machinery operations. WAAFs were not allowed to fly, but it soon became imperative that pilots were available for active duty and not 'wasted' on routine jobs. This led to the formation of the Air Transport Auxiliary (ATA), which was a reserve service that trained and supplied pilots for secondary roles, such as flying aircraft back for repairs or from factories to air bases. Over the six years of war, 150 women flew with the ATA, including the pioneering Amy Johnson, who died on an ATA flight from Blackpool to RAF Kidlington near Oxford in 1941.

The First Aid Nursing Yeomanry (FANY) was founded in 1907, it was an independent female unit and registered charity associated with, but separate from, the army. FANYs were active in both nursing and intelligence work during World War One and in the early 1940s, about 2,000 FANYs undertook espionage work for the Special Operations Executive (SOE). Their highly dangerous jobs involved being sent into enemy-occupied territory and working as saboteurs, couriers and radio operators. About another 2,000 women, specially selected for their intelligence and reliability, were employed at the Government Code and Cipher School at Bletchley Park in Buckinghamshire. There they learned to use the Enigma machine through which they deciphered German secret codes.

The backbone of Britain

While many women were joining the armed forces, many others worked in industries that were normally the realms of men. Their lives were changing irreversibly yet they faced the changes and hardships with determination, humour and a sense of reality. Most women had to do everything in the home that they had always done, plus the jobs that men had traditionally done, such as changing plugs, paying bills, decorating and household repairs. As with all other contingencies, the government provided leaflets giving tips and guidance on dealing with these unfamiliar issues and situations, and magazine articles also offered a plethora of friendly advice.

A huge strength in the fight against Hitler and in keeping up morale was the development of numerous voluntary organisations. As most men of working age were in the armed forces, most voluntary organisations in Britain were full of women. The WVS was one of the biggest. In the prelude to war in 1938, the Home Secretary, Sir Samuel Hoare started the Women's Voluntary Service for Air Raid Precautions to help in the expected air attacks. When war broke out in September 1939, it already had 165,000 members. Wearing their distinctive green and maroon uniforms, they soon began helping in many other areas, and their name was changed to the WVS for Civil Defence. As younger women usually worked in factories or joined the Forces, the WVS was made up predominantly of older women from all social backgrounds. They worked tirelessly and cheerfully, helping and organising, moving into areas and situations where they were really needed and generally forming the backbone of Britain. From the start, the slogan for the WVS was: "the WVS never says no" and their work was diverse. For instance, during the Blitz, London WVS members supplied tea and refreshments to people sheltering in the tube stations and to fire fighters while they cleared up after bombing raids. They organised salvage collections and passed second-hand clothing to those who needed it and they organised knitting and sewing circles, making items of clothing such as socks, jumpers and balaclavas for servicemen. They made glue and fertilisers out of leftover food bones that no one else wanted. They gathered hedgerow fruits to make jam and vegetables (with permission) from the gardens of those who had been evacuated, to give to men in minesweepers and small naval craft who were at sea for long periods and unable to get fresh vegetables. In winter, they added cakes and mince pies to their donations. They made bandages out of old sheets and pyjamas and hospital gowns for the wounded. In 1939 and 1940; they were pivotally involved in assisting with the evacuation of one and a half million mothers and children. Some members ran canteens and rest centres for those who had been bombed out of their homes and many others helped out in public air raid shelters and set up mobile first aid and refreshment centres where they were needed. Betty King remembered:

"My mum was a member of our local WVS. She worked very hard, doing all sorts of things. Most of the time she worked in a canteen that had been set up in an empty shop and cooked and served there on several days a week, from early until late. Anyone would go in, but it was mainly for servicemen and women to have somewhere to go to buy snacks and drinks in warm, friendly surroundings. My mum was also involved with the Soldiers, Sailors and Airmen's Help Society that helped anyone in the Forces needing any help, from financial assistance to health advice. Although she still looked after my brother and me, my mum nearly always worked seven days a week in some capacity for the WVS. Even when she wasn't working in the canteen, she would be altering clothes for the clothing exchange or knitting or darning!"

WVS duties included:
1. Organising salvage collections, including removing iron railings and collecting clothes and aluminium and passing clothes and other essentials on to those whose homes had been bombed.
2. Harvesting rose-hips, which were subsequently used to make a vitamin-enriched syrup which was then given to mothers and children.
3. Setting up and running Incident Inquiry Points after air raids to help anyone affected with such things as finding emergency refuge or medical assistance or liaising in searches for missing people.
4. Setting up rest centres and mobile canteens to provide refreshments for Civil Defence workers and civilians affected by the bombing.
5. Visiting the elderly who might be confused or distressed by the air raids.
6. Initiating and implementing the re-homing gift scheme, which was the finding and arranging of temporary accommodation after people had been bombed out of their homes.

7. Organising evacuation and the billeting of evacuees.

8. Giving advice on nutrition, growing food and the cooking of rationed food or how to cook without gas or electricity after air raids.

9. Providing food and clothing for those who most needed them.

10. Staffing hostels, clubs and communal feeding centres and undertaking welfare work for troops.

11. Organising clothing exchanges of donated clothes (usually from the USA), especially of children's clothes where they could be exchanged for larger sizes as they grew.

12. When American troops began arriving in Britain in 1942, the WVS ran 200 "British Welcome Clubs" across the country.

The AFS, NFS and VAD

Many women helped out with the voluntary Auxiliary Fire Service (AFS), which was formed at the outbreak of war to assist professional fire fighters during air raids. In August 1941, the name was changed to the National Fire Service (NFS), when regional Fire Brigades and the AFS were merged. After that, many more women joined and official uniforms were issued. By March 1943 there were 32,200 women in the NFS, most employed part-time as they also had other occupations. Women's roles in the NFS included working on the switchboard; training new recruits; driving petrol-filled tankers through fires and bomb-blasted streets to re-fuel fire engines; driving canteen lorries to badly bomb-damaged sites, where they administered hot drinks, snacks and encouragement to firemen.

Before the war, it had been unheard of for married women to work, but from 1941, once registered with the Ministry of Labour, many women returned to jobs they had done before they married, such as teaching or nursing. Nurses, of course, were especially needed and those who were qualified were strongly encouraged to return. Eleanor Samuels worked as a nurse in Whitechapel for most of the war:

"I often worked on night duty. When there were air raids, we all ran to push all the beds into the centre of the ward, so if there was any flying glass, it would hopefully miss the patients. Even though it was so horrific, we all laughed a lot and I saw some wonderful acts of kindness and friendship. Everyone helped each other and even the patients, as long as they weren't completely infirm, helped where they could. There were a few miseries, but you get those anywhere! On the whole, we all kept smiling – everyone helped each other."

Meanwhile, untrained but willing women were sent on short, three-month training courses with the Voluntary Aid Detachment (VAD). This organisation, which had been founded in 1909 with the help of the Red Cross and St John's Ambulance, provided nursing services across Britain and the rest of Europe to augment the professional nursing services. To become a member of a local VAD, men and women had to have certificates in first aid. At first, VADs were simply used as auxiliaries; cleaning wards, helping to wash patients, administering bed baths and bed pans and so on, while professional nurses did the 'real' nursing. Eventually, the escalating numbers of patients meant that VADs had to do a lot more and many proved to be particularly competent, even though to begin with they were often resented by the nurses, but interaction improved as the war continued. Some VADs worked in other essential roles, such as cooks, clerks, laboratory assistants and x-ray operators. Sheila Atkinson remembered her time in the VAD:

"I joined the VAD in 1942 when I was sixteen and was sent on a three-month nurse's training course. Immediately after that, I was sent to a hospital in Coventry as a night nurse. I worked five nights a week from 9pm to 5am, with a wage of £5 a week. The National Health Service didn't exist until 1948 and so in those days there were two types of hospital. Voluntary hospitals were dependent on subscriptions, donations by companies and payment for treatment by private patients. Local authorities funded the other type of hospitals, which were called infirmaries and had quite poor reputations. I was lucky enough to work in a voluntary hospital, but conditions were still very hard and I was permanently exhausted. We only got one night off a week and three days every three months, but despite the tiredness and the horrific injuries we tended and upsetting sights we saw, we all kept each other going and when the war was over I missed the feeling of camaraderie."

In total, over the war period nearly 350,000 women served as nurses and first-aiders.

Land girls

In July 1939, the Women's Land Army (WLA), which had been formed in 1917 during World War One, was re-formed. At first, women were asked to volunteer, but later they were enlisted. In 1941, there were 20,000 "Land Girls" as they became called, and within three years, there were 80,000. Working on farms and in forestry, the WLA was crucial as Hitler's U-boats prevented essential supplies from reaching Britain. For a while, Britain was in real danger of being starved into submission, but the work undertaken on the land by women from all walks of life and in all parts of the country changed that around. As with the armed forces, advertising for Land Girls portrayed glamour and a healthy lifestyle. In reality, the work was hard and usually done in isolated and primitive conditions. Land Girls, the majority of whom had never experienced such work and were often not strong, sowed, hoed, drove tractors, milked cows, looked after livestock, thatched, gathered crops and more. Their determination to learn and to succeed was remarkable and their contribution to the war effort was enormous. Called the Land Army because of their tight rules and regulations, most women were employed directly by farmers and were paid a minimum of £1 2s 6d a week. They lived in hostels on the land where they worked and usually had one week's holiday a year. In winter, they worked up to 48 hours a week and during the summer, up to 50 hours a week. As about one third of the Land Girls across Britain came from London, Middlesex or northern industrial towns, it was a huge culture shock for many, but their efforts have become legendary. June Warren had just left school when the war broke out:

"In early 1940, I joined the Women's Land Army because I wanted to live in the country. I'd grown up in Edgware and was longing to experience wide open fields and big skies and to work with animals. First my uniform arrived. It was awful! Khaki coloured breeches that laced at the knees, so bending my legs was difficult. There were also knee length woollen stockings, brown leather shoes, shirts, green jumpers, a broad leather belt and other dull items, including overalls and Wellington boots. My mum was heartbroken when I left, but I thought it was a big adventure. It wasn't quite that! For the first few months I felt very homesick. Our hostel – a wooden hut in a field – had basic amenities: showers, a bath and toilets, a kitchen and common room and a dormitory with bunk beds. There wasn't much privacy. The work was repetitive and heavy and the hours were very long. Hoeing, ploughing, milking, harvesting and building hay ricks were just some of our responsibilities. Our hands were always dry and sore, our backs and legs always ached, but we wouldn't give up. The farmer thought that we 'townies' weren't skilled or strong enough to do the jobs properly, but we proved him wrong!"

WLA hostels' house rules included:
- Punctuality at all times.
- Intoxicating drinks were banned.
- No food could be taken into dormitories at any time.
- "Lights out" was at 11pm every night, with girls in by 10.30, except two late passes were allowed during the week, one until 11pm (lights out in that case at 11.30 or midnight on Saturdays).
- If girls intended to spend a night away from the hostel or to be absent from a meal, they had to inform the warden beforehand.
- Lighting candles or smoking in dormitories was forbidden.
- A House Committee was elected by girls in each hostel. It consisted of five members who each served on the committee for six months.
- Land Girls were urged not to draw attention to themselves with noisy or thoughtless behaviour.
- Any Land Girl's time in residence could be terminated by the warden or other organisers of the Land Army.

Essential work

For the first time ever, women were taking on men's jobs, previously considered to be too physical or complicated for them. Many were operating heavy machinery, turning lathes, stoking boilers, making weapons and shells, or plane or tank parts. Approximately 100,000 women worked on the railways, in jobs such as carriage cleaners, porters, ticket-collectors and mechanics. Another 100,000 worked in the Post Office, while others worked in shops and factories and as plumbers, electricians, chimney sweeps, drivers (of lorries, ambulances, buses and other necessary vehicles). Women proved to be far more resilient, adaptable and able than most had anticipated. In 1942, in a morale-raising exercise, Clement Attlee, then Deputy Prime Minister, made a speech in the House of Commons. Part of it particularly encouraged female workers:

> "This work the women are performing in the munitions factories has to be seen to be believed. Precision engineering jobs which a few years ago would have made a skilled turner's hair stand on end are being performed with deadly accuracy by girls who had no industrial experience."

As the war continued, many women were working for about 80 hours a week, or even longer in aircraft factories. Shifts of 12 hours a time, seven days a week were not unusual and there were few holidays.

With men away fighting, female workers were indispensable. One out of every three workers in the factories was a woman, yet most women earned significantly lower wages than their male counterparts. The majority accepted this. Personal rights were usually put aside in the knowledge that everyone was 'in it together' and 'there's always someone worse off than you'. Nevertheless, many women still realised how undermined they were. Generally, unskilled male workers earned more than skilled female workers. In 1943, in a shocking move (for the times), women at the Rolls Royce factory in Glasgow went on strike. The public made them feel they were being exceptionally unpatriotic and when they were on a street demonstration, they were pelted with rotten eggs and tomatoes – until those pelting them realised just how little they were being paid. The women soon returned to work and were paid slightly more, but it was still less than their male equivalents. It was usual for women to earn half or occasionally two-thirds of the salaries of men. In 1944 the government set up a Royal Commission "to consider the social, economic and financial implications of the claim of equal pay for equal work." Two years later, the Commission's report gave reasons why women earned less: they were not as strong as men and they only worked (outside of wartime) before they were married. Overall during the war, most women accepted lower pay, as winning the war was of paramount importance. Individual disgruntlement was considered selfish and anyway, most women were earning more than they had done in peace time and they had more independence than ever, for which they were grateful. It may be difficult for those living in the twenty-first century to comprehend the strength of patriotism and selflessness of the time. Meanwhile, advertising posters urged people to work harder. Using emotive, fictitious imagery such as "Phyllis Brown" in Britain gossiping over a cup of tea, while "Paula Braun" in Germany carries on working, or "Mr Coleman" going home early, while "Herr Kaufmann" keeps working, government propaganda kept people feeling guilty and so working harder. But despite the rules, lack of freedom and feelings of inadequacy, the sense of unity remained strong. Mary Hollings, who lived in Southampton for most of the war, remembered the collective attitude:

"Despite the worrying news and threats, we took the war in our stride and made the best of circumstances which could have been so much worse. There was an overpowering feeling of accord that we have got to stand together to win this war – we would not be overwhelmed as the French had been. We felt stronger and more independent because we were an island and news of the courage and daring of our Air Force made us even more determined not to let the enemy beat us. During air raids, we made sure we had plenty of the famous British 'stiff upper lip' and certainly did not show any fear or panic. Indeed, while bombs were dropping all around us, most women I knew did their knitting."

Humour played a huge part in keeping up morale during the war. Tales of laughter and foolishness are often relayed by those who were there despite the atrocities they were experiencing and hearing about. The government tried to keep morale buoyant with rousing speeches and optimistic messages and newspapers printed jokes and cartoons.

Worker's Playtime

The Entertainments National Service Association (ENSA) was initially established by the government to brighten the lives of those in the armed forces and later, civilians. Over 80 per cent of all British dancers, musicians, singers and actors belonged to ENSA. Many were heard on the BBC's Home Service and Forces programmes in live broadcasts. The three most famous female singers of the period were Vera Lynn, Gracie Fields and Anne Shelton, who sang of hopes for a happier world. Vera Lynn became known as the "Forces' Sweetheart", visiting troops serving abroad and releasing songs that inspired both civilians and servicemen and women. In 1941, she launched her own BBC radio show called *Sincerely Yours*, where she read out messages from loved ones, connecting those fighting abroad and those at home. Her songs: *We'll Meet Again* and *The White Cliffs of Dover* spread hope and happiness and made her the most popular female entertainer in Britain. The simple tunes of the most popular songs in the war were often churned out in sing-songs in air raid shelters or around dinner tables across Britain.

Long shifts meant that all workers tired. From June 1940, the BBC began broadcasting the radio programme *Music While You Work*. Featuring two half-hour sessions of continuous popular tunes each day, it was played over tannoys in factories and businesses throughout the country, something that had never happened before. From 1942, a night programme was broadcast for shift workers. Before the war, the BBC had been accused of being dull, but during the war it gained a new lease of life and became exceptionally important to the British. The upbeat tunes on *Music While You Work* helped to lift everyone's mood and to keep them working. Any tune that included clapping or other similar rhythmic beats was not played as it was discovered that it distracted listeners and disrupted their output. The following year, in June 1941, the BBC introduced *Worker's Playtime*, a revolutionary new radio show. Broadcast live from a secret factory canteen "somewhere in Britain", it was a comedy and music programme, one of the first touring variety shows on the BBC. Originally scheduled to run twice-weekly for six weeks, it continued for 23 years and became one of the longest running radio shows in history. Short on excitement and things to smile about, audiences appreciated even the corniest of comedians, but there were also some genuinely funny acts along with the more mediocre. The government fully supported the programme as it brightened everyone up. The Ministry of Labour chose which canteens the show would visit and broadcast from. Periodically, Ernest Bevin the Minister of Labour and National Service, who had been one of the instigators of the programme, spoke to offer his encouragement to workers.

Other forms of entertainment included the cinema (picture palace) and theatre, or dancing. Dance halls and cinemas were diverting, lifting the moods of all those who attended. Most plays and films were uplifting realism or escapism. *Gone with the Wind* from Hollywood opened in early 1940 and continued to run throughout the war. American films were far more colourful and exciting than the more earnest and lower budget British films, but all films were greatly enjoyed and cinemas – of which there were several in every town – developed into a huge business, attracting 25 to 30 million paying customers every week. Every town and village throughout Britain also had a hall where dancing could take place. Church and school halls often doubled as dance halls too. Larger dance halls had orchestras; smaller ones often had a three-piece band, someone playing a piano or a record player. Being together in a well-lit hall, with lively music helped many forget the suffering, shortages and perils of the war for a short time. Mirrored balls in the centre of the ceiling scattered beams of magical light or coloured spotlights created a bright glow. Most halls had chairs and tables around the walls. As there was a shortage of men, girls often danced with other girls, but everyone knew all the main dances. During the first few years of the war, these were the waltz, foxtrot, quickstep and samba. Then, between 1942 and 1945, more than one and a half million US servicemen moved to Britain. Among other things, they introduced the jive and the jitterbug, which although outrageous to some, caught on immediately. It was incredibly lively, fast and exciting. Soon everyone was twirling, spinning and throwing each other about on dance floors across the country. Dancing was also an excuse for women to dress up and to feel feminine once more after the stringent rules of their working days, where the majority wore uniforms or overalls and had to scrape their hair under turbans or hats.

The art of war

At the end of December 1939, the government set up the CEMA, the Council for the Encouragement of Music and the Arts, which after the war became the Arts Council. In the same year, it also set up the War Artists Advisory Committee (WAAC), led by Kenneth Clark. Art during wartime was viewed by the authorities as a necessity, to raise everyone's mood. The WAAC encouraged artists to produce works that focused on heartening themes of heroism, patriotism, energy and defiance and travelling art exhibitions were set up across London and other locations across Britain, including factories and military bases. A total of 400 WAAC official war artists were selected; 52 being women and all invited to propose ideas. This was the first time that females were officially encouraged to capture their impressions of war. The WAAC sent artists on paid short-term commissions. There were still considerable inequalities between female and male artists; male artists were given more important commissions, more pay and greater publicity. But amateur artists also made sketches, capturing their perceptions of what they saw in factories, at the shops and in air raid shelters, for instance. Such unofficial drawings were discouraged however; as the authorities tried to control war imagery to ensure that no negative ideas emerged. Yet most of the art produced by women war artists was vivid and forceful, capturing the realities of life at home and how war was affecting the ways in which they lived and worked. Some of the most famous artists of the period were Dame Laura Knight, Anna Airy and Margaret Abbess. Their creative and insightful portrayals depicted salient aspects of life on the Home Front during some of the darkest hours, but remained emotive and inspiring.

A woman's place

Despite the enormous changes to everyone's lives, with disruptions caused by women working outside the home, the shortages and rationing, the separations and fears, regular life had to continue. Many young women – and men – were lonely, anxious and not sure what was ahead of them. The war prompted a surge in marriages, but also a boom in illegitimate births. These babies were usually born in nursing homes and adopted within a few days. With no social security and plenty of social taboos, there was little else young unmarried women could do. Additionally, with husbands and wives separated for lengthy periods, the temptation to stray was often strong. Whatever happened, in the main, it remained women's responsibility to maintain the home, as mothers, wives and daughters; cooking, cleaning, shopping, caring for everyone and generally making sure that home life was as close to 'normal' as possible. Advertising posters, government leaflets and magazine columns were all intent on giving advice and helping to build a sense of solidarity between the women of Britain and in general, they spurred each other on. In 1943, *Good Housekeeping* ran an article, "Danger – men at work". It described how more men, if they were still at home or had returned on leave from the Forces, had to help with the housework and to adapt to women being altered through their wartime experiences. The tongue-in-cheek article commented on men feeling themselves to be "victims of circumstance" who could barely recognise their newly independent wives who could now hold down men's jobs and undertake household repairs while continuing to do traditional women's household tasks. But as everyone realised, with their enterprise, strength and courage and their determination to succeed, the war changed women's lives irrevocably.

3
NO BANANAS

"Many people are still unaware that the greatest profession or business is that of housekeeping. There are more people daily employed in it than in any other form of work. In wartime, housekeeping becomes even more important than in peacetime. If those who keep house went on strike, the war would be lost in a week." ~ Good Housekeeping, 1942

Before the war, about 60 per cent of food was imported; Britain only grew enough to feed one person in three. Yet on 9th September 1939, the new Minister of Food, William Morrison stated in *The Daily Telegraph*, that there were 'splendid stocks of food in the country, and there was no need to fear any shortage. Within a short time however, when Hitler realised invasion would not be possible, he aimed instead to starve Britain into submission. German U-boats frequently attacked and sank supply ships trying to reach British shores and from June 1940, the Germans also occupied the Channel Islands, effectively cutting off the last of Britain's supplies. Stocks of staple goods such as tea, sugar, fruit, coffee and even rubber, were particularly scarce.

Initially, after the experiences of World War One, Morrison had reckoned that the rationing scheme would come into operation by October 1939, not through scarcity, but because "food had to be fairly and evenly distributed". Ration books had originally been printed in 1938 but as it turned out, they were not used until January

1940 (and continued in use until 1954). Most people actually welcomed rationing, as the severe shortages impinged adversely on nearly everyone, except the rich who were hardly affected and had been able to stock up on most goods. Rationing was run extremely efficiently and made everything fairer. Nevertheless, long queues still formed outside shops that were rumoured to have received fresh supplies of any items.

Ration books
Everyone was issued with a ration book allowing them to buy a limited amount of certain foods. Adjustments were made to cater for special needs, like pregnant women, young children and vegetarians, but even so, parents often relinquished some of their food rations to their children to keep them healthy and strong. People registered with their local shops and, as items were bought, the shopkeeper stamped their ration books or, later on, accepted small paper coupons from the books. The first items to be rationed were butter, sugar, bacon and paper, followed closely by meat, tea, jam, biscuits, breakfast cereals, cheese, eggs, lard, milk and tinned fruit. Bread, potatoes, coffee, vegetables, fresh fruit and fish were never rationed, though availability and choice of the last three were often severely limited. Bread and potatoes became the principal bulk items in everyone's diet and the government launched advertising campaigns to encourage healthy eating – especially among children – using these more readily available foods, based on the characters "Potato Pete" and "Doctor Carrot". Created into cartoon characters and featuring poems and songs, the campaign was a popular one. For instance, a poster featuring Potato Pete gave people ideas for using potatoes freely:

Potatoes new
Potatoes old
Potato (in a salad) cold
Potatoes baked or mashed or fried
Potatoes whole, potato pied
Enjoy them all, including chips
Remembering spuds don't come in ships.

Exotic fruits like bananas, grapes, peaches, melons and lemons were not available at all throughout the war and most children born during it or very young at the start, never tasted bananas until it was all over. (A popular song in 1943 was called *When can I have a banana again?*) Tea was the main beverage of the nation and when it was rationed at the rate of two ounces a week, which made barely two cups a day, many felt demoralised – even more so than with the rationing of other foods. As it was considered so important to public morale, the government rationed it carefully to make sure it would last. Many hoarded their tea rations, drank it weaker or kept it warm in flasks to take to the bomb shelter. Rather than throw the precious substance away, even leftover cold tea was reheated and drunk later. Acknowledging the drink's popularity, Winston Churchill said, "Tea is more important than bullets." Some tried tea substitutes, such as pouring boiling water on dried apple, pear cores or nettles, but these were intensely disliked. Coffee, although not as popular as tea at the time, was often replaced by substitutes made from various roasted grains. Acorn coffee became infamous as something the Germans enjoyed, so acorn coffee did not take off in Britain, but Camp Coffee essence, made with chicory was at least British and so became a fairly successful product. The magazine *Country Life*, which frequently featured articles on recipes and nutrition, ran a piece on substitutions, including: "A note on nettle tea: nettles can be used satisfactorily as a vegetable, for nettle tea and soup, even when in flower."

Rationing entitlement varied at different times and further items were added as they became increasingly difficult to obtain. In November 1941, a points system was applied to breakfast cereals, condensed milk, biscuits, canned meat, fish and vegetables, allowing housewives to choose between various goods, which were each given a fixed points value. Under this system, each person had 20 points which had to last for four weeks. The points system gave people a degree of choice; for example, a tin of soup was six points, a tin of fruit 24 points and condensed milk 10 points. By 1945, half of all Britain's food was rationed. People often saved their coupons to buy particular things (for instance, children frequently saved their sweet rations in order to buy a larger amount at once – and many children bought boiled sweets that lasted longer than say, chocolate). Most rationing was dictated by weight, but some things, such as meat, were rationed by price. Sweets and chocolate, although sharply reduced in variety, were rationed in a different way again. Everyone had 'personal points', which could be spent anywhere, without registration and these points or sweet coupons were cut out by the shopkeeper, who then tied a batch together and handed them over in return for his or her next delivery of sweet supplies. Grumbling occurred, but not usually over the rationing. Instead, grievances were mostly about the unavailability of goods that were not rationed. Women frequently queued for hours outside shops where it was heard that certain food items were available, but many were still sent away disappointed and numerous shops only opened on a few days a week as their stocks sold out so quickly and were not replenished quite as speedily.

Black market

Although ration books were precious commodities usually held on to vigilantly, by 1943 the government estimated that 700,000 had been lost or stolen. Inevitably perhaps, an illegal black market flourished where certain individuals sold difficult to obtain items secretly at high prices or favoured customers were sold rare items from – literally – under the counter. Perhaps even more inevitably, many of these illicit goods were not what they promised to be. The Ministry of Food employed staff to investigate these illicit dealings secretly and the government passed legislation to enable the courts to impose fines of up to £500, with a possible two years' imprisonment. Ultimately, nearly 1,000 inspectors were employed by the Ministry of Food for these investigations. The MP Joseph Clynes described the black market when the country was facing such hardships as "treason of the very worse kind" and others in the House of Commons joined him in calling for the government to introduce even stronger punishments for black market offences.

An example of an adult's weekly rations in 1943:
3 pints of milk
3¼lb-1lb meat
1 egg (or 1 packet of dried eggs every two months)

3-4oz cheese
4oz bacon and ham
2oz tea
8oz sugar
2oz butter
2oz cooking fat
16 points a month for other rationed foods, subject to availability

Rations were extremely meagre by contemporary standards. For instance, two ounces of tea is equivalent to about 20 teabags. Three to four ounces of cheddar cheese would probably be eaten as a snack today. With hardly any households containing fridges or freezers, convenience foods during the war were mainly tinned or bottled items, such as spaghetti, ravioli, baked beans, peas, soups, potatoes, custard, creamed rice, fruit, Carnation milk and salad cream. Sauces, pickles and relishes were in short supply but not rationed, as were pastes, some biscuits and jellies. Housewives tried to stock up with these as well as with nerve tonics and comforting beverages such as Horlick's, Ovaltine, Rowntree's, Bournvita, Bourneville or Fry's cocoa.

Better nutrition
It is generally accepted that food rationing improved the nation's health. Pre-war surveys showed that a quarter of the British population was undernourished, infant mortality was at a high rate, 80 per cent of under-fives had some bone abnormality and 90 per cent had badly formed or decayed teeth. As the shortages continued, people became used to eating less food, less fat and sugar and more vegetables. Officials calculated the minimum nutritional requirements for everyone and planned rationing accordingly, issuing different coloured books to suit different requirements. Buff-coloured books were given to most adults; green books were given to pregnant women, nursing mothers and babies and children under five. They were allowed the first choice of fruit, a larger allowance of fresh orange juice, a daily pint of milk and a double supply of eggs, while blue ration books were issued to children between five and 16 years old, who were allowed fruit, the full meat ration and half a pint of

milk a day. On 8th December 1941, the government introduced the Vitamin Welfare scheme, to make sure that all children got the vitamins they needed to stay healthy. Children up to the age of two were given free cod liver oil and blackcurrant syrup. In 1942, the blackcurrant syrup was replaced with orange juice and the scheme was extended to include expectant mothers who were later also allowed Vitamin A and D tablets if they could not tolerate cod liver oil. This care of the nutrition of babies and children was considered to be of the utmost importance; as Churchill had said in 1943: "There is no finer investment for any community than putting milk into babies."

Fair payment and allocation

Rationed goods still had to be paid for and in 1941; the Ministry of Food implemented comprehensive new price controls across the country to prevent retailers from making excessive profits on foods that were in short supply. That June, the Ministry also introduced 'controlled distribution' of eggs as rural areas had a greater supply of eggs and other farm produce than town-dwellers. For the course of the war, the government took over the organisation of all food provision and supply to retailers. All importers, manufacturers, wholesalers and retailers worked under the direction of the Ministry of Food, which acted for the benefit of the country as a whole. To this end, local Food Control Committees were set up to look after the interests of consumers and to supervise retail distribution. Shopkeepers were licensed to trade by these committees and instructed not to supply excessive quantities to any customers, while similar powers were taken to prevent people from buying too much. Maximum prices were fixed by the Ministry for most foods and displayed in shop windows.

In it together

The government promoted rationing and economy as a moral, nationalistic issue, with posters declaring that while waste in peacetime cost money, waste in wartime cost lives. It all amounted to greater originality and creativity being needed by those who provided meals at home. "Better pot-luck with Churchill today than humble pie with Hitler tomorrow", "Be thankful and never grumble" and "Never leave any food on your plate" ran contemporary advertisements. People – particularly housewives – rose to the challenge with resourcefulness, sacrifice and enterprise. Rather than being crushed by the difficulties, in place of deprivation there developed a shared sense of camaraderie and fighting spirit; a united approach to making the restrictions a reason for innovative thinking and creative cooking. A glut of recipe books was published to accommodate shortages of the most basic ingredients. Wherever they appeared; in magazines, newspapers, leaflets, books or advertisements, all recipes were designed to encourage wives and mothers to extract as much nutritional value as possible from the limited variety and amounts of food available. The Ministry of Food produced information leaflets on nutrition and cooking, such as *A Kitchen Goes to War* in 1940, in which famous people contributed 150 recipes that could be prepared using rationed foods. The famous contributors included Lady David Douglas-Hamilton, Lady Milne-Watson, Margot, Countess of Oxford and Asquith, the chef of the Savoy hotel, Agatha Christie, Rebecca West and Stella Gibbons. These people were all known to the public from the society and celebrity pages of daily papers, and the objective of the leaflet, coming so early in the war, was to reinforce the idea that everyone was in it together. The recipes aimed to help housewives avoid boredom with the limited ingredients available, but most were not particularly exciting! For instance, Agatha Christie contributed a recipe for Mystery Potatoes, which were simply potatoes mashed with anchovies. In addition, short educational films were shown at cinemas and the BBC launched a daily morning radio programme called *The Kitchen Front*, which featured plenty of facts, recipes and advice. Various presenters of cooking came to the fore. Two sisters, Elsie and Doris Waters were a successful comedy double act and stars of radio and stage. Better known as the Cockney duo "Gert and Daisy" they wrote their own comic songs and sketches and made several films for the Ministry of Food. They also produced *Gert and Daisy's Wartime Cookery Book*, which was a great success as they were so popular. Other wartime cook books included *Meals without Meat*, *Potato Pete's Recipe Book*, *McDougall's Wartime Cookery Book*, *The Stork Wartime*

Cookery Book, Try Cooking Cabbage this Way and *We'll Eat Again*. Cooking demonstrations by well-known cooks such as Marguerite Patten were held in many large stores across the country. Mrs Patten joined the Ministry of Food in 1942 to advise families on how to manage rations and gain the maximum nutritional value from the food available. Her brief was to 'inspire people' and among many things, she tried to persuade adults to eat raw, grated turnip as a valuable source of vitamins. All the information given to the public was intended to instil confidence in (mainly) women who were unsure about how to provide varied, nutritious meals on what little they could get, how they could alleviate hunger on meagre rations and how to stretch the limited ingredients further than they realised they could.

Inspired by necessity, everyone faced the challenges with resolve and made do with less, or substituted ingredients with the unusual or unexpected. In April 1940, William Morrison became Minister of Shipping and Lord Woolton became Minister of Food, remaining in the job until December 1943. Lord Woolton was determined to improve the nutritional value of the British diet and for the first time the findings of nutritional science, which had been researched since about 1914 were applied to feeding the population. The subsequent food policy promoted both adequate nourishment and the economical use of available foods. Under Lord Woolton's direction, a new government advertising campaign was promoted; reminding everyone not to waste food, and giving further nutritional information and recipe suggestions. (Prosecutions for wasting food were not unknown.) As the campaign was launched, Lord Woolton published an initial message that outlined the government's aims:

"Here is your part in the fight for Victory. When a particular food is not available, cheerfully accept something else – home produced if possible. Keep loyally to the rationing regulations. Above all, when you are shopping, cooking or eating – remember, 'Food is a Munition of War. Don't waste it.'"

The Ministry of Food arranged for supplies of sugar to be delivered to various women's voluntary organisations, such as the

Women's Institute, the Townswomen's Guild and the WVS. So that British-grown fruit was not wasted, the sugar was used for making jam. The Ministry of Food also urged everyone to substitute accessible ingredients where others were scarce, such as potato pastry in place of the usual pastry made of flour and grated potatoes in place of suet. Sour milk was suggested to be used instead of cheese; grated raw vegetables could replace fruit and whipped margarine with vanilla flavouring was suggested as an adequate substitute for cream. Oatmeal was another ingredient people were encouraged to eat more of, which was quite new to those living in the south of the country and carrots were used as a sweetener for all sorts of recipes, including steamed puddings, cakes and carrot jam. Other creative attempts at making mundane, repetitive ingredients tasty and diverse included pounding, mincing and marinating.

Scornful of some of the suggestions for menus and recipes using rations, Winston Churchill wrote to Lord Woolton: "The way to lose the war is to try to force the British public into a diet of milk, oatmeal, potatoes etc., washed down on gala occasions with a little lime juice." In another incident, when Churchill heard that people were complaining about the meanness of their meat ration, he asked to see it. Not realising that he was being shown a week's allowance, he assumed it was for just one meal and remarked that it would be quite enough for him!

For those living through the war who had not had the privilege of cheap package holidays, wartime recipes were far plainer than we are used to. Careful planning was always advised and recipes included many stock-cupboard ingredients that rarely included exotic spices. Apart from an occasional shake of nutmeg, cayenne pepper and generic curry powder, there was little in the way of seasoning beyond salt and pepper and white sauce was often recommended, while sweet dishes were often flavoured with condensed milk or golden syrup instead of sugar.

Examples of wartime recipes

Here are a few of the dishes offered to wartime housewives in magazines, leaflets and newspapers.

Railway pudding

6 oz flour
3 oz margarine or dripping
2 oz sugar
1 egg
A little milk
1 teaspoon baking powder
Pinch of salt

Sift the flour with the baking powder and a pinch of salt. Rub in the fat, add the sugar and mix with the beaten egg and about four tablespoons of milk. Put in a greased pie-dish and bake in a moderate oven for about 30 minutes. Serve with warmed jam on top.

Potato Jane

1½ lb potatoes
3 oz grated cheese
2 oz breadcrumbs
½ chopped leek
1 sliced carrot
½-¾ pint milk or water
Salt and pepper

Put a layer of sliced potatoes in an ovenproof dish. Sprinkle with some of the leek, carrot, crumbs, cheese and seasoning. Fill the dish with alternate layers, finishing with a layer of mixed cheese and crumbs. Pour over the milk and bake in a moderate oven for 45 minutes or steam for 1 hour.

Carrot cookies

½ lb carrots
3 tablespoons of sugar
2 tablespoons of cooking margarine
5 tablespoons of self-raising flour

Cream together the margarine and nearly all the sugar, keeping back a dessertspoonful. Grate the carrot and beat it into the margarine and sugar. Fold in the flour lightly until the dough is soft and creamy. You can add a tablespoon of water if the carrots are dry.

Drop spoonfuls of the mixture into greased patty pans. Sprinkle the tops with the extra sugar. Put into a moderate oven and cook for about 25 minutes.

Potato scones

6 oz flour
4 oz mashed potato
1 teaspoon baking powder
½ teaspoon salt
1 oz fat
4-5 tablespoons milk
Mix the flour and salt. Add the baking powder and work into the mashed potato. Rub in the fat. Blend to a soft dough with milk. Roll out to ¼ inch thickness. Cut into rounds. Brush the tops of the scones with milk. Bake on greased baking sheets for 15 minutes in a hot oven. For a sweet scone add 1oz sugar.

Clear soup

2 pints clear stock
1 carrot
1 turnip
1 oz butter
1 small piece of celery
1 leek
1 onion
Salt
Shred the vegetables. Melt the butter in a pan and cook the vegetables until they are slightly brown. Boil the stock and season to taste, add the vegetables and cook till tender. Remove scum as it rises. Add shredded lettuce, boil for a few minutes and serve.

Potato Floddies

Scrub two potatoes and grate with a coarse grater over a bowl, then add sufficient flour to form a batter and season with salt and pepper. Melt a little dripping and make very hot in a frying pan. Drop the mixture into it. When brown on one side turn and brown the other. Serve with jam if you want it as a sweet dish or, if you prefer it as a savoury, add a pinch of mixed herbs and a dash of cayenne pepper.

Steamed chocolate duff

6 oz flour
¾ teaspoon baking powder
2½ teaspoons cocoa
2½ teaspoons sugar
1½ oz fat
1½ oz grated raw potato
Milk and water

Rub the fat into the flour and mix all ingredients together. Make into a soft dough with the liquid and then steam in a small greased mould for about 30-40 minutes.

Victory sponge

1 large raw potato, finely grated
2 medium raw carrots, finely grated
1 breakfast cupful breadcrumbs
1 tablespoon self-raising flour
2 tablespoons sugar
½ teaspoon vanilla or lemon flavouring
1 teaspoon baking powder

Mix all the ingredients together, then coat the inside of a heated basin with 2 or 3 tablespoons of jam, allow to cool and fill with mixture. Tie on a cover of greased paper, steam for 2 hours.

Steamed chocolate pudding

2 oz margarine
1 oz sugar
1 cup grated carrot
2 tablespoon golden syrup
2 cups plain flour
1 teaspoon bicarbonate of soda
1 teaspoon baking powder
1 heaped teaspoon cocoa
Pinch of salt
½ pint milk
A little vanilla essence

Peel and grate the carrot. Cream the margarine and sugar together until pale and fluffy and then stir in the grated carrot, syrup and

*the rest of the dry ingredients. Add the milk and a few drops of
vanilla essence and mix it all to a fairly stiff consistency. Grease a
basin and put the mixture into it. Cover with greased baking paper.
Tie string around the paper and basin. Put the basin into a large
pan of boiling water, put a close-fitting lid on top and steam for two
hours. Do not let the water in the bottom of the steamer boil dry. To
test, put a fork or skewer into the centre of the pudding. Like a cake,
if it comes out clean, the pudding is ready.*

Pepping things up

Without fridges, wartime housewives had to visit their local shops
each day to buy fresh food as it was impossible to store this for more
than a day or two. Most households kept milk, butter and other such
foods in larders and bowls of cold water. Because so many recipes
were somewhat uninspiring, flavourings in the form of sauces, pickles
and gravies were recommended to enliven them. Such products
included Bisto (invented in 1908 with the slogan, "Browns, Seasons
and Thickens all in One"), Vita-Gravy, Oxo and Bovril. Many brands,
included recipes in their advertising, for example, McDougall's flour
advertised a "mock beefsteak pudding" and a Bovril headline ran:
"Little cubes of carrot, leeks and 'taters too, simmered with some
Bovril, make a beefy stew." Usually a more detailed recipe was
included, for example:

Vegetable hotpot

*Peel and slice about a pound of mixed vegetables – carrots, parsnips
and a small swede make a good variety, with a leek or an onion if
possible. Do the same with 1lb potatoes. Melt 2oz dripping in a
casserole, add all the vegetables, season well and fry lightly. Make
½ pint of stock by dissolving one dessertspoonful of Bovril in boiling
water. Pour over the vegetables and cook for about 1½ hours in a
moderate oven.*

Among many other things, in the 1940 book *101 Things to Do in
Wartime,* by Lillie B. and Arthur C. Horth recommended keeping a
stockpot going, using any bones, trimmings and other leftovers,
covered with boiling water and boiled up each day, to use as a base

for other dishes. The authors suggested that vegetables were not put in the stockpot or they might turn the liquor sour. Suggestions for flavourings in the book included celery seeds, tied up in muslin; with pulses including peas, beans and lentils, added for extra protein.

The mother of invention

Despite the restrictions, shortages and monotony of the ingredients available, several dishes were invented out of necessity during the war that have since become classics, such as fruit crumble, which replaced full pastry cases for fruit pies and carrot cake when carrots were used as substitutes for apricots and sugar.

Dry bread and dried eggs

Before the war, white bread had been a British staple, usually spread lavishly with butter and jam. From 1942, difficulties in obtaining white flour created a crisis – white bread could no longer be provided for everyone in the country. In its place, a standard wholemeal loaf made with "national wheatmeal" flour of 85 per cent extraction with added calcium and vitamins was introduced. In March, Lord Woolton announced that no more white bread would be sold after 6th April 1942 and instead the national wheatmeal loaf would take its place. This coarse, grey, hard-crusted loaf was so unpopular that people nicknamed it "Hitler's Secret Weapon". In truth, the wholemeal bread was far more nutritious than white bread, particularly when butter was in such short supply as well.

In terms of restrictions and rationing, 1941 was the most difficult year of the war. The individual adult meat allowance dropped to one shilling per person per week, fish escalated to over four times its pre-war price, cheese became rationed (although vegetarians, miners and farm workers were allowed extra) and even onions became scarce. In June of that year, eggs were rationed too. Each adult was allowed approximately three eggs a month, with children under five, pregnant women and nursing mothers allowed double that. The following summer, controlled supplies of powdered egg were made available, easing things a little. One packet of dried eggs, equivalent to 12 fresh eggs, was allocated to each adult approximately every eight weeks.

Dried egg, which arrived from the USA, was greeted with mixed feelings. Most disliked the rubbery texture, but it was another shared element that gave people further opportunities to bond with each other. *The Ministry of Food War Cookery Leaflet No. 11* gave instructions for reconstituting dried egg, plus several dried egg recipes. Although many complained about them during the war, once dried eggs had disappeared after the war, even more people protested that they wanted them back! An article in *Good Housekeeping* magazine in November 1943 with the baseline: 'The Ministry of Food has approved this article,' was called 'Dried Eggs'. Written by Nora Ramsay, it began:

> "Dried eggs are one of the best foods that wartime rationing has brought us. Always available, always fresh and ready to use, they help the cook in a hundred ways. More than that – they provide every member of the family, from one year old up, with valuable body-building extras for the winter months."

The article gave instructions for reconstituting dried eggs, by mixing the powder to a smooth cream with a small amount of water, then stirring in further water to make a runny consistency. Recipes included:

Egg and potato fritters
1 large raw potato
1 dried egg
Dripping or bacon fat (for frying)
1 tablespoon flour
Salt and pepper
Milk if necessary
Put the flour, egg and seasoning into a basin and mix thoroughly. Peel the potato, then shred with a coarse shredder into the flour. Make a hollow in the centre of the ingredients and, if necessary, stir in milk to give a thick batter. Drop spoonfuls of the mixture into hot bacon fat or dripping, and fry gently until browned, then turn and fry the other side. Serve immediately. Diced cooked bacon or cold cooked sausage can be added to the fritters if available.

Sadie Belasco used dried egg to make her simple cheese omelette:

Sadie's cheese omelette
4 dried eggs made from 4 level tablespoons dried egg and 8
tablespoons water
Salt and pepper
2 oz grated cheese
½ oz margarine
Reconstitute the egg and add seasoning. Heat the fat in a pan, pour
in the egg and work the mixture with a fork. As the egg is setting,
sprinkle in the grated cheese and cook for one minute longer. Fold
and serve hot with a garnish of watercress or other fresh green
vegetable.

The lend-lease agreement
After 1941, the British navy managed to destroy more German U-
boats and the "lend-lease" agreement with America came into effect,
making food availability a little less strained. After Churchill had made
the plea to the US of: "Give us the tools and we'll finish the job" the
lend-lease agreement began; a system whereby the USA sent
munitions and food parcels to Britain, the latter containing such
things as tinned sausage meat, cheese, soya flour, corned beef, Spam
(which stood for Supply Pressed American Meat) and dried eggs.
Payment for this was deferred until after the war. Although extremely
welcome, the lend-lease scheme was not without problems. Corned
beef, Spam and dried eggs had not been sold in Britain before and
housewives were not sure what to do with them and it was not easy
to ration the food as the amounts sent varied and arrived in Britain
erratically. Various recipes to use these unfamiliar products were
published, by the Ministry of Food and by respected cooks or
individuals, such as:

Grace Palmer's Corned Beef Hash
Gently fry a large chopped onion or leek. Peel, slice and cook four
potatoes and two large carrots, or some swede, and cut corned beef
into thick slices. Layer these ingredients in an enamel pie dish. Make
a rich gravy using Bisto or Oxo and pour this over all the

ingredients. End with a layer of sliced potato and sprinkle grated cheese over the top. Bake in an oven on a low heat for 20 minutes. Serve with green vegetables or baked beans.

Corned beef pie
(from 101 Things to Do in Wartime)
Grease a pie dish and place ½ lb of sliced tomatoes in the bottom. Cut 1 lb of corned beef into dice, moisten with a little good, cold gravy, add pepper and salt to taste, place this on the top of the tomatoes and sprinkle a generous helping of chutney or Pan Yan pickle on top. Cover with mashed potatoes, with knobs of dripping or margarine dotted on top. Cook in a fairly hot oven for about half an hour.

The Ministry of Food's Spam Fritters
12 oz can of Spam
Margarine for frying
4 oz plain flour
Pinch of salt
1 large egg or the equivalent of dried egg
4 fl oz milk, or milk and water, or beer
Mix together all the batter ingredients in a bowl. The mixture should be thick, to coat the Spam well. Cut the Spam into eight slices. Meanwhile, heat the margarine in a frying pan; coat the Spam slices once or twice with the batter then drop them into the hot margarine. Cook for two to three minutes on each side, turning over the fritters as required.

Jackie Watson, who lived in Kensington and Penzance during the war, remembered the large tins of American sausage meat, which cost a vast 16 ration points and was more wholesome and tastier than Spam. The meat was surrounded by a thick layer – nearly half a pound – of fat, which was invaluable for cooking and a more appetising alternative to the liquid paraffin some recipes suggested to be used for fat.

Eating out
Meals eaten away from home, whether in expensive restaurants or industrial canteens, were not counted as rations and became a

popular alternative with those who could afford them. Individuals who worked away from home and could afford to do so often ate in cafés and canteens, which meant that their rations were saved. To ensure that everyone was adequately nourished, 'British Restaurants' were set up by the government, in actual restaurants, evacuated schools or even church halls, where workers could get a hot meal at a modest price. Minced beef with carrots and parsnips was a typical dish. Other restaurants carried on as they had before the war. But many who were suffering the financial strains of the war resented the rich being able to continue eating in these expensive restaurants. To try to balance the situation, from 1942 the government prohibited all restaurants from charging more than five shillings a meal and no meal could consist of more than three courses, which helped, but did not stop the problem completely. Less expensive restaurants such as the Lyons Corner House chain remained accessible to all throughout the war. Dependable and reasonably priced, they became popular gathering places. With some branches still opening and providing hot meals even after extensive bomb-damage, Lyons gained the reputation that they were fighting the war and facing adversity along with everyone else, which reinforced their popularity. Numerous makeshift canteens and cafés were set up by various voluntary groups throughout the war, including the WVS and the Salvation Army and by local authorities. These cheaper and convenient eating places served members of the Forces, firemen, shift workers, the public in air raid shelters, or in particularly bomb-damaged areas. A variety of different premises were used for this, including schools, empty shops and church halls.

Festive fare

In 1943, even the sugar coating on pills was stopped. If everyday provisions seemed dull, the choices for festive fare seemed even worse and housewives inventiveness, while taking into account the government's slogan of "waste not, want not" was stretched to the limit. As ever, the Ministry of Food tried to help, printing and broadcasting recipes that could be managed with the shortages that were deemed suitable for wartime celebrations, and each Christmas housewives were allowed some extra items in the weeks leading up to it, to help families to celebrate as best they could and to boost morale. Everyone listened to the radio carefully for announcements of what extras there would be. The Ministry of Food also ran editorial pieces in newspapers and magazines and distributed regular food facts leaflets containing recipes and encouragement, for instance in the weeks before Christmas in 1943, it stated: "We can still make Christmas fare hearty, tempting and appetising to look at. Here, with our very best wishes, are some ideas which may help you." These were some of the ideas:

Mock Goose

1½ lb potatoes
2 large cooking apples
4 oz cheese
½ teaspoon dried sage
salt and pepper
¾ pint vegetable stock
1 tablespoon flour
Scrub and slice potatoes thinly; slice apples, grate cheese. Grease an ovenproof dish, place a layer of potatoes in it, cover with apple and a little sage, season lightly and sprinkle with cheese, repeat layers leaving potatoes and cheese to cover. Pour in half a pint of the stock, cook in a moderate oven for 45 minutes. Blend the flour with the remainder of the stock, pour into the dish and cook for another quarter of an hour. Serve as a main dish with a green vegetable.

Christmas Day Pudding

Rub three ounces of fat into three tablespoonfuls of self-raising flour until it resembles fine crumbs. Mix in one and a half cupfuls of stale breadcrumbs, half a pound of prunes (soaked for 24 hours, stoned and chopped) or any other dried fruit, such as sultanas. Add three ounces of sugar, one teaspoonful of mixed spice, one teaspoonful of grated nutmeg, then chop one large apple finely, grate one large raw carrot and one large raw potato; add to dry ingredients. Stir in a tablespoonful of lemon substitute. Mix one teaspoonful of bicarbonate of soda in three tablespoonfuls of warm milk and stir thoroughly into the pudding mixture. Put into one large or two small, well-greased basins, cover with margarine papers and steam for two and a half hours. This can be prepared overnight and cooked on Christmas Day.

Emergency Cream
(Most people scooped the top of the milk off and collected it to have a little cream, but this recipe was widespread for making 'mock' cream.)
Bring half a pint of water to blood heat; melt one tablespoonful of unsalted margarine in it. Sprinkle three heaped tablespoonfuls of household milk powder into this, beat well and then whisk thoroughly. Add one teaspoonful of sugar and half a teaspoonful of vanilla, leave to get very cold before serving.

Syrup Loaf
Cooking time: 30 minutes
Quantity: 1 loaf
4 oz self raising flour, or plain flour with 2 teaspoons baking powder
½ teaspoon bicarbonate of soda
Pinch of salt
2 tablespoons warmed golden syrup
¼ pint of milk, or milk and water
Method:
1. Sift flour (or flour and baking powder), bicarbonate of soda and salt.
2. Heat syrup and milk (or milk and water), pour over the flour and beat well.
3. Pour into a well greased 1 lb loaf tin and bake in the centre of a moderately hot oven to cook for 30 minutes or until firm.

Christmas cake
½ lb margarine
½ lb sugar (brown if possible)
5 dried eggs
10 tablespoons water
½ teaspoon almond essence
½ teaspoon vanilla essence

¾ lb plain flour
1 level teaspoon bicarbonate soda
½ level teaspoon
Salt
2 level teaspoons mixed spice
2 lb mixed dried fruit
3-4 tablespoons ale, stout, or milk
Cream the margarine and sugar, adding the dried eggs and water
gradually. Beat until white and creamy. Add the essences, sift the
flour, soda, salt and spices together and add to the mixture. Add the
prepared fruit and lastly the liquid to make a fairly stiff mixture.
Mix thoroughly and put in a cake tin lined with paper. Bake in a
slow oven for three hours and leave in the tin to cool.

Icing

4 level dessertspoons sugar
6 level tablespoons dry milk powder
2 tablespoons water
Colouring and flavouring
Mix the sugar and milk together, add water and beat until smooth.
Add colouring and flavouring and spread on top of the cake.
Alternatively, it was suggested that eight melted marshmallows
made an adequate substitute as icing for a Christmas cake.

4

DIGGING FOR VICTORY

"We want not only the big man with the plough but the little man with the spade to get busy this autumn... Let 'Dig for Victory' be the motto of everyone with a garden" ~ Rob Hudson, Minister for Agriculture, October 1939

Before the war, Britain imported over 55 million tons of food a year. The ships delivering these provisions were some of the first targets of the German U-boats. By early 1941, shortages were at their worst when merchant ships travelling to British shores were being sunk at a rate of three a day. The slogan that had been used by the Ministry of Agriculture since 1939 to encourage people to grow their own food; "Dig for Victory", had never been so important.

For many years before the war, gardening had been a popular pastime in Britain, especially among people who had moved out of the cities and into the new suburbs. Vegetable growing had been taken up by a few, but mainly men; women rarely became involved. Once World War Two became imminent, everyone in Britain was encouraged to take to their gardens and grow their own food. Anyone with a private garden was advised to turn it into a mini-allotment to provide essential crops for themselves and their neighbours and to help the war effort in general. Vegetable-growing was to be done by all as it was imperative that the British merchant navy changed its role and became available for transporting troops and munitions rather than food. More food grown at home meant ships could concentrate on bringing in vital arms. One ad ran: "To be sure of the family's vegetables, you must grow them yourselves – women and older children as well as men. If you haven't a garden, ask your Local Council for an allotment. Start to Dig for Victory Now!" The message was acknowledged and within a few months, even the public parks, formal public gardens and areas of unused land in Britain were transformed into vegetable plantations. Tennis courts, cricket and football pitches and golf courses were ploughed up, although there was an outcry when it was suggested that Wimbledon's courts were going to be dug up. The long dried-up moat at the Tower of London became an allotment; the flowers in Kensington Gardens were replaced with rows of cabbages; the Great Park at Windsor became the biggest cornfield in Britain; sheep grazed in Green Park, and Hyde Park had its own piggery. Even the soil that covered Anderson shelters was used by many to grow cabbages, marrows, cucumbers and rhubarb. In an effort to become rapidly self-sufficient, the government also encouraged people to keep a few chickens or ducks to supplement their egg rations. Some communities set up pig clubs, with groups of neighbours buying one or two pigs between them, feeding the pigs on kitchen scraps and sharing the pork when the pigs were slaughtered. It became quite a craze, as 900 pig clubs were eventually set up. Barbara Matthews remembered:

"You needed somewhere for pig sties, a source of available food, and men willing to take turns in cleaning out the sties."

Goats were also kept by some for milk and rabbits were reared for stews. By 1944 a quarter of the official production of eggs came from domestic sources and around 6,000 animals were kept in private gardens. As part of the curriculum, pupils cultivated vegetables in their grounds, with the crops used to supplement their school dinners. The food-growing exercise was so successful that by 1943, over a million tons of vegetables were being grown in British gardens and allotments. At the same time, farming was modernised and the Women's Land Army was providing much-needed labour for the growing agricultural sector.

Propaganda

Aware that the British people were in danger of being starved into submission as so much imported food came from Canada and America and supplies coming across the Atlantic were particularly vulnerable to German attack, the government had to work decisively. In October 1939, the Minister of Agriculture, Sir Reginald Dorman-Smith had announced on the radio: "Half a million more allotments properly worked will provide potatoes and vegetables that will feed another million adults and half a million children for eight months out of twelve....So, let's get going, let 'Dig for Victory' be the motto of everyone with a garden and of every able-bodied man and woman capable of digging an allotment in their spare time." Soon after, the head of the Agricultural Plans Branch of the Ministry of Food, John Raeburn, set up the Dig for Victory campaign, which the Minister of Food, Lord Woolton, exploited enthusiastically. While much of the credit for the campaign went to Lord Woolton, Dorman-Smith had instigated it and John Raeburn ran it from 1941 throughout the war and was responsible for its continuing success. Through pamphlets, books, newspaper articles and "food flashes", which were short, instructional films shown before feature films, the government made sure that the public knew how to prepare soil, plant seeds and harvest the crops. The first food flashes came across as stern and moralising, and were heckled in cinemas, they were soon adjusted by the Ministry of Information who made them, and later films featured cartoons and humour. The Dig for Victory campaign stimulated public enthusiasm. Audrey Sykes remembered:

"We all grew marvellous crops. Shallots, onions, leeks, cabbages, carrots and potatoes; there was no manure and no expensive equipment available, but every space, from railway sidings to window boxes were suddenly blooming with the tops of growing vegetables – it was quite a work of art. If anyone had any spare time, they spent it growing veg!"

The BBC also rose to the challenge once more with its 'Radio Allotment' vegetable plot, which grew 23 varieties of vegetables and from which weekly reports were broadcast, informing listeners about developments, discoveries and progress. The first gardening celebrity, Cecil Henry Middleton, began broadcasting on the BBC Home Service in September 1940. He became a national treasure, known by all as Mr Middleton. "These are critical times," he said, "but we shall get through them and the harder we dig for victory, the sooner will the roses be with us." The son of a head gardener in Northamptonshire, Mr Middleton originally contributed to a gardening column for *The Daily Express*, persuading thousands to take up their spades. Even before the war, he had a huge following with his weekly radio programme *In Your Garden*. Relaxed and friendly, showing his empathy with amateur gardeners and an astute sense of humour, he spoke as if his listeners were close friends, and frequently referred to his own gardening failures and successes, arousing a sense of shared problems and camaraderie. It was a great contrast to the formal style broadcasts people were used to. He advised about seed sowing, planning crops, dealing with difficulties and he advised on what to do in the garden or allotment during every week of the year. *In Your Garden* was broadcast on Sunday afternoons throughout the war, attracting 3.5 million listeners, with advice such as:

> Buy good tools – Do not borrow, buy. Choose a good [spade] with an "all-bright" blade if you can find such a treasure. Look after it, keep it clean and sharp and it will last for years.
> Dig wisely – Now comes a word of warning. Do not break your neck over this digging. Digging is what you make it, a painful, back-aching ordeal or a pleasant recreation, and if you are not used to it, it should be taken as medicine, in small doses.

Mr Middleton's amusing and encouraging comments included: "An allotment is like the army. The first month is the worst. After that you begin to enjoy it" and "Keep your tools clean and bright. No man can dig properly with a dirty spade" or "Step on the spade instead of the accelerator. You'll reach your journey's end quicker."

Growing tips
In the book *101 Things to Do in Wartime*, there are tips on mushroom growing. It explains how "mushrooms can be grown all the year

round in places where no other crops will grow, such as cellars, dark sheds, garages and even in spare rooms inside the house." Readers were advised to "provide a number of boxes to a convenient size having a depth of six inches or so." The boxes could be arranged in tiers or in rows and the compost was to be spread on the trays to a depth of five inches and allowed to settle. The mushroom spawn should be broken up and planted at intervals and the compost covered with a thin layer of ordinary soil. "An infrequent very light watering is applied, but never in sufficient quantity to seep through the boxes and apart from keeping the beds free from weeds and away from draughts, no other attention is needed. When gathering the mushrooms, they are twisted from the bed – not cut – and the disturbed soil smoothed over. The stems are then cut off about three-quarters of an inch from the cap."

In the same book, ideas about arranging a vegetable garden were given: "Try a border of carrots with cabbage lettuce behind. Further back, alternate with ordinary and spinach beet with clumps of rhubarb and plants of ordinary and button tomatoes behind; the contrasts of colour being most effective. If there is room, an effective background can be provided by a row or two of Brussels sprouts."

A food war

Particularly through Lord Woolton's charm, business acumen and understanding of the British psyche (he spoke to women about the various difficulties as if they were his daughters, which endeared him to them), the Dig for Victory campaign was a success, and prevented the British from starving during or after the war. In ensuring that everyone was educated about growing and preparing nutritious food, Woolton created an "all in it together" attitude and helped to increase the nation's collective determination to remain strong. Over ten million instructional leaflets were distributed and it was estimated that by 1945, over 1.4 million people had allotments, producing more than a million tons of vegetables a year and the acreage of British land used for food production increased by 80 per cent. In 1941, Lord Woolton had declared: "This is a food war. Every extra row of vegetables in allotments saves shipping... the battle on the kitchen front cannot be won without help from the kitchen garden." Advertising was particularly effective in heartening and inspiring the public. Copywriters and art directors who designed and wrote the ads knew how to persuade and unite people. Strong images, simple slogans and occasional cheerful and jovial humour efficiently conveyed the idea that the nation was working as one and persuaded all to take responsibility for themselves and others as far as they could. These same Ministry advertisers devised characters such as Potato Pete and Doctor Carrot which helped to popularise two of the most widely available foods. The characters, displayed in iconic posters in stations, shops and offices, in leaflets and recipes, and in specially written songs and slogans, became extremely popular. It was an inspirational campaign accomplished with great success, using marketing techniques far in advance of their time. Through radio advertising and colourful posters in particular, the songs tapped into the public enjoyment of having a good old sing-song to cheer themselves and each other up.

> The Dig for Victory song
> Dig! Dig! Dig!
> And your muscles will grow big
> Keep on pushing the spade
> Don't mind the worms
> Just ignore their squirms
> And when your back aches, laugh with glee
> And keep on digging
> Till we give our foes a wigging
> Dig! Dig! Dig for Victory!

Other ads and editorial issued by the Ministry of Food, made helpful suggestions, such as: "Fruitful results from vegetables" which appeared in *Good Housekeeping* in 1942. It began:

> "Eating fruit is a pleasure we don't often get nowadays, and there's no denying we miss it. But, from the point of view of health, we can more than make up for the lack of fruit by eating extra vegetables. The main health value of fruit is in the vitamin C. Vitamin C clears the skin, prevents fatigue and helps you to

resist infection. And it's by no means confined to oranges as people are apt to imagine. Some vegetables, indeed, actually contain more of the health-giver than oranges do."

Doctor Carrot

Doctor Carrot was featured in magazine articles and posters to instruct people about how many different ways they could use the healthy and versatile vegetable. Perhaps because Doctor Carrot looked a little old-fashioned with his wing-collar and top hat, Disney in America invented the slightly more modern Clara Carrot. Both proclaimed cheery sayings, such as "I'll put pep in your step", "I'm an energy food" and "Doctor Carrot guards your health". Culinary delights such as curried carrot, carrot jam and a home-made drink called Carrolade (a blend of carrot and swede juice) were just some of the Ministry's suggestions for making use of carrots. Two other recipes that helped to satisfy a sweet craving were:

Carrot Fudge

4 tablespoons finely grated carrot
1 leaf of gelatine
Orange squash
Cook the carrot in just enough water to keep them covered for ten minutes. Add some orange squash to the water. Melt the leaf of gelatine and add this to the carrot and orange mixture. Cook this again for a few minutes, stirring the mixture all the time. Spoon into a flat dish and then leave it to set. Cut into cubes.

Treacle Toffee Carrots

½ lb sugar
½ lb treacle
1 tablespoon vinegar
2 oz margarine
A handful of fresh carrots
Melt the margarine in a strong saucepan and add all the other ingredients except the carrots. Bring to the boil and keep boiling steadily until a little if the mixture, when dropped into cold water

immediately becomes brittle. Wash and scrape the carrots, then dry them thoroughly, dip them into the toffee as soon as it reaches the brittle stage and pour the rest of the toffee into a greased tin to set firm.

The slogan "Carrots keep you healthy and help you see in the blackout" was one of the particularly successful ways that the government promoted carrots quite shamelessly. It was made known that the carotene or vitamin A in carrots was largely responsible for the RAF's increasing success in shooting down enemy bombers. In reality, carrots are important in keeping eyes healthy, but they do not miraculously enhance anyone's vision, in the dark or otherwise. The myth was strengthened when a Royal Air Force pilot, John Cunningham, gained a remarkably good record of shooting down enemy planes at night. Nicknamed "Cat Eyes", Cunningham declared that his love of carrots was the reason for his phenomenal night vision. As a result, people ate carrots enthusiastically, believing it would help them to see more clearly in the blackout. It was important for all to incorporate vegetables into their regular diets, so the idea worked well, but the main reason for the RAF's success was the British advances in the use of radar. Besides, most people ignored the fact that Dr Carrot wore glasses!

Potato Pete

As well as carrots, potatoes were promoted fervently as a beneficial and accessible source of protein and energy. As with the Dig for Victory song, Potato Pete also had his own song augmenting his message. Recorded by the actress Betty Driver, it helped to popularise potatoes even more. Potato Pete recipe books were published with suggestions and advice on how best to serve the vitamin and mineral-rich vegetable and the Ministry of Food's *War Cookery Leaflet No. 3* focused on potatoes. It began:

"There is no vegetable more useful than the homely potato. Potatoes are a cheap source of energy, and they are one of the foods that help to protect us from illness. They contain the same vitamin as oranges and ¾ lb of potatoes daily will give over half the amount of this vitamin needed to prevent fatigue and help fight infection…don't think of potatoes merely as something to serve with the meat. They can be much more than that. A stuffed, baked potato can be a course in itself. Potatoes can be used, too, for soups, bread-rolls, pastry, puddings and even cakes."

To cut down on waste and retain the most nutrients, scrubbing rather than peeling potatoes was recommended in the leaflet:

1. Always cook them in their skins
2. If you must peel them, peel thinly
3. After peeling, cook at once. Avoid soaking in water if possible

And in a more child-friendly poem:

'Those who have the will to win
Cook potatoes in their skin
Knowing that the sight of peelings
Deeply hurts Lord Woolton's feelings.'

To popularise potatoes with children, even some traditional nursery rhymes were adapted to Potato Pete themes, for instance:

There was an old woman who lived in a shoe.
She had so many children she didn't know what to do.
She gave them potatoes instead of some bread,
And the children were happy and very well fed.

In April 1943, Lord Woolton announced: "We had better use our intelligence and the knowledge we have. We can now produce meals without meat in them, and they will keep us well and give us all the energy we need to keep us fighting fit." As ever, there were many educational leaflets produced to help, including: *Onions and Related Crops, How to Make a Compost Heap, How to Sow Seeds, Pests and Diseases in the Vegetable Garden* and *Preserves from the Garden*. Towards the end of the war, the government also distributed a monthly *Allotment and Garden Guide*, which gave practical tips such as:

> "If the weather be fine in February, we shall be anxious to get onto the vegetable plot. Never work the soil when it is too wet and sticky...seeds sown in cold, wet soil will rot instead of germinating. Remember when ordering your seeds that half a pint of runner beans will sow a row 50 feet long."

The Ministry of Agriculture *Dig for Victory Leaflet No. 1*, focused on a "Cropping Plan for a 90' x 30' Plot" and "Grow Vegetables All Year Round", which began:

> "Vegetables for you and your family every week of the year. Never a week without food from your garden or allotment. Not only fresh peas and lettuce in June – new potatoes in July, but all the health-giving vegetables in WINTER – when supplies are scarce...savoys, sprouts, kale, sprouting broccoli, onions, leeks, carrots, parsnips and beet. Vegetables all the year round if you dig well and crop wisely."

The leaflet continued with "Allotment or Garden Layout and Schedule of Crop Rotation", which included a table, showing where and when vegetables and fruit should be planted and how to rotate them for the best results. People were advised to grow what they enjoyed eating. The core crops that people grew were: potatoes, carrots, turnips, peas, parsnips, beets, leeks, cauliflower, runner, dwarf and broad beans, shallots, tomatoes, onions, marrows, kale, radishes, parsley, cabbages, Brussels sprouts, swede, lettuces, spinach and sprouting broccoli. Stan Bell remembers his family's garden in Loughborough, where they grew peas, rhubarb, cabbages, potatoes and carrots. "All the children helped to grow things. I grew dwarf beans on canes, thinking they were climbing runner beans, but dwarf beans weren't climbers. They grew anyway and they were delicious!" Efforts were made by everyone to recycle and to manage the land responsibly. To this end all sorts of organic practices were advised. The main objective was to produce abundant crops with the highest nutritional content. One of the Ministry of Agriculture's leaflets explained how to cultivate fresh vegetables throughout the year in: "Grow for winter as well as summer." Alf Bailey, who was eight when the war broke out and lived in East Anglia from 1942 to the end of the war, recalled:

"Our allotment was ten minutes' walk away from our house. There were about twenty or thirty allotments on the same land. I used to go there with my dad (who was a fireman) on most evenings in the summer after school and on Saturdays and Sundays during the winter. We mainly grew vegetables and some fruit. My job was weeding and picking. Everything was seasonal then – in winter we grew and ate root vegetables and in summer we grew and ate lettuces and radishes. We grew some fruit – we had some blackberry and red currant bushes and some rhubarb. When it was ripe, I picked the fruit, collecting it all in a saucepan and took it home for my mum. She often made it into a crumble for Sunday dinner and sometimes she made jam."

Peter Evans remembered helping his mother on their allotment: "We used all sorts of household objects, like toilet roll tubes, cardboard boxes and egg cartons for germinating seeds and growing small plants, then when they were big and strong enough, we moved them to the soil." Jack Baker's father collected old windows and made them into cold frames, growing spinach, kale and lettuce under them. Other original ideas included covering vulnerable young plants with old net curtains to prevent birds and insects from eating them. Children usually helped by digging, planting, weeding and picking the produce. Some children worked on farms in the school summer holidays, picking the fruit and vegetables.

In addition to all this, recipes for the free food that could be found around the countryside were published and distributed, promoting such dubious dishes as crow pie, braised sorrel, nettle salad and squirrel-tail soup. Housewives were advised to make jams, chutneys, preserves, purées and pickles from wild berries, other hedgerow fruits and the leftovers of the fruits and vegetables they grew. Cooked nettles were said to taste a lot like spinach and rosehips made a tasty and nutritious soup.

Woolton Pie

Lord Woolton's charisma was such that even after advising people to make rissoles without beef, cakes without sugar and tea without tea leaves, he remained a popular figure. Among the many different – and often dull dishes – that the Ministry of Food suggested, a vegetable pie was developed named after him, invented by the chef of the Savoy hotel and utilising the produce grown by so many. It was not liked and jokingly nicknamed by some as "steak and kidney pie without the steak and kidney!" Lord Woolton fully endorsed it for its health content:

> ### Woolton Pie
> *1 lb diced potatoes*
> *1 lb cauliflower*
> *1 lb diced carrots*
> *1 lb diced swede*
> *3/4 spring onions*
> *1 teaspoon vegetable extract*
> *1 tablespoon oatmeal*
> *A little chopped parsley*
> *The ingredients of the pie can be adapted to fit whatever vegetables are available. Potato, swede, cauliflower and carrot make a good mixture. Cook all the ingredients together for ten minutes with just enough water to cover. Stir occasionally to prevent the mixture from sticking. Allow to cool and then put it into a pie dish, sprinkle with chopped parsley and cover with a crust of potato or wheatmeal pastry. Bake in a moderate oven until the pastry is nicely browned and serve hot with a brown gravy. This makes enough for four or five.*

Farms and allotments

As well as many areas of wasteland, parks, playing fields, railway embankments and back gardens being cultivated, a large number of farms were extended, with approximately 10 million acres of grassland being ploughed up to be used as arable land. The extension of farms meant that the farmers had to make far greater investments in time and machinery. Since the outbreak of the war, every county had a committee made up of Ministry of Agriculture officials and the National Farmers' Union to oversee and control the farming. The committees had great powers and their aim was to increase production. They controlled every aspect of farming, including which crops were grown, the number of workers needed, permits for machinery purchase, fuel distribution and so on. Because the farmers on the committees were usually highly respected, the committee system was quite friendly and on the whole instigated the sharing of information and ideas. It was not unknown however, for committees to evict farmers who could not or would not comply with the imposed greater demands on their time and expenditure. Whatever the difficulties by 1944 Britain had increased its area of arable land by 50 per cent, its pastures by 66 per cent, had nearly doubled its production of wheat and barley, and more than doubled its yield of potatoes.

Sowing the seeds of independence

Under the dynamic leadership of the Marchioness of Reading, the Women's Land Army was re-launched in the summer of 1939, in response to the national drive for agricultural self-sufficiency and the need for land workers. In its aim to attract girls from factories, offices and shops, advertising for the WLA appealed to those who fancied a healthy outdoor lifestyle, but the reality of the work was harsh and strenuous and food was not always as nourishing or as plentiful as it should be. Aged from 18 to 40, land girls across the country worked from early in the morning (milking usually began at 4am) until late in the evenings. In an attempt to correct this over-romanticised view, the publication *Land Girl, a Manual for Volunteers* suggested that potential recruits should test themselves by "carrying buckets of water for half an hour or more at a time", after which they should "attempt to pitch earth on to a barrow...for another hour or so." During their four weeks' training, land girls only received 10 shillings and their keep. This did not improve much when recruited and they had no say in where they would be sent or in what tasks they would be asked to do. Despite the vast majority having no previous experience, of many farmers resenting them and of many being less robust than the male farmhands they were replacing, the efforts made by them all was acknowledged as being extraordinary, and the gruelling and physically demanding jobs they succeeded in doing helped to increase Britain's food production massively. Their work was hugely diverse, from looking after animals and ploughing fields, to harvesting crops and killing rats, to digging, hoeing, shearing and milking. On top of this in the main, they had to learn to use old-fashioned methods and equipment.

As one of the consequences of the heavy, outdoor work was hunger, extra rations were allocated to land girls, but the food they were given was often inadequate. As their uniforms also wore out quickly, they were supplied with cheap, second-hand clothes and when their rubber boots wore out, as rubber was in short supply, they were returned for reconditioning and sold back to the girls, off-ration and at a cheaper price. Some of the girls were billeted on the farms where they worked; many lived together in hostels and they were all moved as and when they were needed by the War Agricultural Committee. To join the WLA, girls were interviewed, then given a medical examination and then enrolled. The official minimum age for enrolment was 17, but some lied and joined at 16 or even younger. It was not difficult to be admitted as there was so much work to do. Although pay was quite low and there was no holiday entitlement, there were certain perks. If a girl was working over 20 miles from home, once she had worked six months, she was granted a free journey home, paid for by the government. It was left to the farmers' discretion to allow their workers any other time off.

The Squander Bug

Faced with so many shortages, any form of unnecessary wastage was strongly discouraged. In one of his many broadcasts to the nation, Lord Woolton said: "If you are only eating what you need and not what you like and as much as you like, then you are helping to win the war." People were encouraged to save kitchen waste for their own or their neighbours' pigs or hens, or to give it to the local authorities who collected it for their livestock. Promoted by the government,

70

advertisers invented the "Squander Bug" as the opposite of the friendly Doctor Carrot and Potato Pete. The Squander Bug looked like a giant flea or large beetle, with German swastika symbols all over his body and Hitler's hairstyle. He was always trying to tempt people into wasting food, money and other essentials. Posters, newsreels and pamphlets warned of the dangers of extravagance and wasting things that could ill-afford to be frittered away. The Squander Bug tempted housewives to spend more than they should and headlines proclaimed: "Kill him – with War Savings" or "Don't take the Squander Bug shopping with you". Newspaper ads of 1944 implored: "Don't let the Squander Bug nibble at your will to save. Whenever he raises his ugly head, squash him. The need to save is as urgent as ever. Save to finish the war and speed the peace. Save in your own interest so that you will have money to spend with a good conscience when there are more things in the shops." Posters and slogans appeared everywhere to remind people of the need to save as much of everything as they could. Extravagance was deplored. The campaign worked and by April 1943 31,000 tonnes of kitchen waste were being saved every week, which was enough to feed 210,000 pigs. Manufacturers were not exempt from the need for economy and to save paper, metal and labour, most wartime packaging was reduced. Food packaging in particular became plainer and smaller and often carried the words: "wartime economy pack" or "wartime emergency pack".

Various innovations were made by people in their attempts to avoid wastage. Apple peel was boiled to make a lemon substitute for use in jams or drinks; bacon rinds were melted to be used as fat for cooking or were added to soups for flavouring; stale bread went into puddings or to make stuffing or was used as breadcrumbs and added to dishes such as scrambled egg to make them go further. Other scraps were used to feed the animals. But while it was important to save and be cautious, stockpiling food became an offence that was punishable by imprisonment. Leaflets like *What's in the Larder?* gave information on using up leftovers to ensure that nothing was wasted. Tips included:

"Food which has already been cooked only needs to be re-heated and is spoiled if cooked too much a second time. This is especially important to remember when using up leftover meat, fish and vegetables", and:

"Using up Stale Bread: Fairy Toast – cut wafer-thin slices of stale bread and bake in a moderate oven until crisp and golden brown. Store in an airtight tin. This is a good standby to have in place of bread or biscuits and it will keep for months."

In the effort to educate people on growing and cooking, not wasting food and in keeping healthy, the Ministry of Food joined with the Ministry of Agriculture and the Ministry of Education. Along with their unrelenting advertising campaigns and leaflets, they also set up food advice centres in larger towns, run by home economics cookery advisors to recommend ways of doing all these things.

Exceeding all expectations

Of all the Home Front directives, the Dig for Victory campaign was the most successful, exceeding all expectations. In a complete turnaround from the start of the war, by 1945 approximately 75 per cent of the food needed in Britain was produced within its shores. Yet even when the war was coming to an end, the government realised that complacency was not an option and people would need to remain self-sufficient for some time. In a speech in late 1944, Lord Woolton announced: "We can justly congratulate ourselves in what we have achieved. But we must on no account relax out efforts. The war is not yet won. Moreover, even if it were to end in Europe sooner than we expect, the food situation, far from becoming easier, may well become more difficult owing to the urgent necessity of feeding the starving people of Europe. Indeed in many ways it would be true to say that our real tasks will only then begin. Carry on therefore with your good work. Do not rest on your spades, except for those brief periods which are every gardener's privilege." People continued to grow their own food for years after the war. In 1950 there were still approximately 1,200,000 allotments being used but by 1968 there were approximately 600,000. Rationing did not finally come to an end until 1954, with meat being the last food to come off the ration list.

5
YOUR BATTLE ORDERS

"War gives us a chance to show our mettle. We wanted equal rights with men; they took us at our word. We are proud to work for victory beside them. And work is not our only task. We must triumph over routine; keep the spirit of light-heartedness. Our faces must never reflect personal troubles." ~ Yardley advertisement in 1942

Yardley was not the only cosmetic company that told women blatantly to make their appearances a priority during the war. Cosmetic advertising was used almost as propaganda as it was seen as unpatriotic not to try to look one's best. The Yardley ad above continued: "With leisure and beauty-aids so rare, looking our best is especially creditable. Let us face the future bravely and honour the subtle bond between good looks and good morale." Advertisers and beauty journalists constantly reminded their readers that, more than ever, it was their duty to look their best. Most advertising used a rather condescending tone of voice that would irritate many in the twenty-first century, ("match-made for flattery", "a woman's crowning glory" and "sure you couldn't be lovelier if you took more care?") but women of the 1940s were used to and accepted this. Another Yardley ad of the war period ran: "Put your best face forward...To look lovely while you 'look lively' is a big help to good morale, for good looks and a high heart go together." An ad for Elizabeth Arden ran: "Tomorrow takes a bow! Yesterday's self was glamorous – today's is serious and hardworking. Tomorrow's – with the consciousness of work well done – will shine forth in the beauty and gaiety that is every woman's birthright...Tomorrow's self will be a woman whose smile we are proud to receive."

Make-up

It had been realised quite early on in the war that looking good boosted the morale of everyone – and women in particular were urged to look their best when their husbands came home, whether from work or on leave from fighting. So the government tried to encourage them, despite the terrible circumstances, to take care of their appearances as much as they could. Before the war, the wearing of cosmetics had been considered by many as being rather vulgar; anything more than a restrained dab of powder had been disapproved of as not respectable. But once the war started and everything seemed so drab, increasing numbers of women began wearing more make-up. It was a way that they could still feel feminine while they were taking on men's roles. Many of the older generation were shocked to see women in uniform wearing lipstick, foundation and powder, but the heavy make-up worn at first to counteract the effect of severe uniforms did not last long as by 1941, cosmetics became increasingly scarce. In October 1942, an article in *Good Housekeeping* written by Susan Drake was called 'How do you look when he comes home?' Typically for the time, it concentrated on encouraging women readers to make themselves attractive for their men! It ran:

> "...Today when there are so many good excuses to let appearances slide there is no need to search for one. There's the war, the shortage of cosmetics, and there's the one about working so hard there isn't time anyway. But, at the risk of being called frivolous or superficial, I'm sticking to my opinion that a woman's job of keeping herself attractive is as important now as ever it was. This is as true of older women as younger folk... The truth is that economy and a right attitude to wartime conditions should be as nearly invisible as possible."

The fashion for make-up was established and old taboos of disrespectability had almost vanished. Women found it confidence-boosting; a way of making themselves feel better and they did not want to stop wearing it. As the war continued, there was rarely enough stock of anything to be found anywhere, but in an attempt to hold on to some semblance of glamour, many improvised when they could not get hold of essential items.

Simplicity was the key to the application and style, predominantly because there were so few choices of products and colours. Brands available at the start of the war included Yardley, Coty, Revlon, Helena Rubenstein, Max Factor, Tangee, Goya, Dubarry et cie, Snowfire, Dorothy Gray, Boots Number 7 and Elizabeth Arden, but the technology was limited and tastes were restricted; directly inspired by Hollywood. Skin was creamy-pink and powdered; lips were matte red and eyelashes were enhanced with mascara – this came in cake form, with a tiny brush like a miniature toothbrush and required moisture (usually spit) to apply it. Eyebrows were arched and defined. A particular orangey-red lipstick shade by Tangee (priced at 6d) was popular as it contrasted well with the khaki uniforms of the ATS but this soon became scarce, although lipstick continued to be manufactured on a reduced scale throughout the war, as it was considered to be psychologically important. The early metal packaging however, was soon replaced with plastic and then with paper. Pond's cold cream, Vaseline and Vitapointe conditioning cream for hair were the few items usually available throughout the war and these were used extensively. Women constantly checked their local chemists' shops and any new cosmetic supplies were sold out within an hour. Well-known brands were scarce and some enterprising chemists made their own cosmetics such as cold cream, hand cream and talcum powder from simple ingredients. Many women would take their own jugs or bottles to particular chemists who would fill up their containers with home-made creams for a small price. Perfumes were also in limited availability and those that were around were quite strong – effectiveness overcame subtlety. The three perfumes that most women remember were Ashes of Roses and Evening in Paris both made by Bourjois (who also made the most popular rouge of the period) and both sold in Woolworth's and Californian Poppy made by Atkinson. A 1943 ad for Californian Poppy ran: "As haunting as a Chopin nocturne…as dangerous as a

tropical moon…as tantalising as a yashmak…as intimate as a kiss…
as deadly as a live wire…"

By 1940 fabrics were needed desperately for uniforms,
parachutes, hospital blankets and other wartime essentials, so clothes
rationing was introduced. With fashion no longer changing and
developing as it did in peacetime, make-up and hairstyles became
more important in the quest for women to make themselves look
attractive and feel special, but with so many things in short supply, it
was not easy. One afternoon in 1943 the manager of a Ministry of
Labour office in a small Berkshire town gave each of his female staff
permission to take a short break as it had been circulated that a local
shop had received a delivery of hairgrips. The year before the
Ministry of Supply had become so concerned about the morale of
women munitions workers that they distributed an allowance of face
powder and foundation with a booklet called *Beauty Hints, Look to
Your Looks*. At another time, Max Factor officials from America
visited some munitions factories and gave out new pancake make-up
and lipstick. After they had handled a lot of explosive materials,
munitions workers' skin often turned yellow, so they were urged to
wear make-up as a protective barrier against the chemicals and the
dirt they worked with each day. Women in the Forces were allowed
to wear discreet and understated make-up, and in general, most
women eked out products to make them last or hoarded them if they
managed to buy any, but inevitably cosmetics became used up or
dried up over the course of the war.

Some women tried making their own cosmetics. With rationing,
shortages in practically everything and limited availability of
ingredients that might have been helpful, most of these attempts were
not too successful. Calamine lotion was sometimes mixed with cold
cream to create a form of foundation. Powdered starch was used as
face powder and Fuller's earth powder was mixed with water to make
a face mask. Red lips – which became a symbol of patriotism during
the period – were occasionally improvised with beetroot juice and
Vaseline, but although in short supply, lipsticks could still be bought
and most women simply continued to use theirs as sparingly as
possible right to the bottom of every tube. End pieces of lipsticks were
often scooped into egg cups and stood in hot water so that they

melted together and could continue to be used. Eyebrow pencils were devised by lighting a match and then blowing it out and using the soot residue to darken the brow. Some women used shoe polish or burnt cork for mascara. Rouge, which was in powder cake form, was also used as sparingly as possible but if that was used up the old-fashioned pinching method usually had to suffice. Or they followed the tip in a magazine article, which recommended that readers "add a few drops of warm almond oil" to cold cream to make it go further or to melted down lipstick ends to use as a cream rouge. A 1942 advertisement for Ino soap featured the headline 'Powdered Starch and Beetroot Juice'. It began:

"Why worry if cosmetics become so scarce that you are reduced to these primitive substitutes for face powder and rouge! Remember the first aid to beauty – INO Toilet Soap, with its creamy, gently searching lather that penetrates pore-deep, nourishing as it cleanses."

In August 1944 *Good Housekeeping* ran an article by Susan Drake, called 'Kitchen Beauty Calendar'. It was one of many to expound the benefits of using natural ingredients as beauty preparations. The article began:

"1. The next time you prepare tomatoes for the table, wash your hands with some of the parts you normally throw away. Tomato juice whitens the skin.
2. Washing dishes or clothes? Then take time off to wipe off your make-up and cream you face. The cream will prevent the steam from enlarging the pores; the cream-plus-steam will give the skin a pore-deep cleansing. Steamy work over, remove the cream and wipe the face with skin tonic, rose water or complexion milk."

Other magazines gave further suggestions, including:

"1. To fill out hollows in the neck, warm a little olive oil and pat it into the hollow places with your finger tips. Repeat this treatment every night before going to bed.

2. Combing your hair in the sunshine will help to keep it in good condition. Lift up your hair, piece by piece to let the air and sunshine reach the roots.

3. Cucumber is excellent for whitening the skin. Put a few slices of cucumber in a saucer of milk, and let it soak for an hour. Then gently wash the face with the milk and rub the cucumber into the skin. Let it dry on for half an hour, then spray it off with a little rose water. This treatment will be very soothing when the skin has become hot and rough with the sun and wind."

To counterbalance any upset caused by the dearth of beauty products, the government promoted the importance of a clear complexion, declaring that this was far more beautiful than the artificiality of powder and rouge. In a quest for this natural beauty, women were encouraged to eat fresh vegetables and to wash well in good, wholesome soap; which was fine until early in 1942 when soap was rationed. After that, every adult could choose from either four ounces of household soap or two ounces of toilet soap per person per month. This caused major problems. Soap rationing affected personal hygiene, laundry and house washing; most people collected their tiny slivers of leftover soap in a jam jar, which they then squashed together. Magazine articles began featuring soap-saving tips, such as collecting the last pieces of soap in a pan, covering them with boiling water, stirring the mixture over a low heat and then pouring it into a dish to set. The squishy result could be used for a lot longer than the small, leftover scraps of soap. Other ideas included putting the soap scraps into a tin, piercing the tin with several holes and pouring boiling water through – the resulting liquid was a watered-down solution of soap. Chris Butterworth relates how her nan, Emily Adams, "eked out those last little extra-thin slivers of toilet soap that were too small to wash your face with by collecting several of them in the foot of a nylon stocking, knotting them in, and then using that to lather up and wash with." Some families put washing soda crystals into baths in place of coloured bath salts. As it was, water had to be used with care. It was recommended that only one bath a week was taken and hair should only be washed at the most once a fortnight. And on top of that, razor blades were practically impossible to obtain.

Hair care

Even though women's salaries were lower than their male equivalents, wartime work for women meant that most still earned more than they had previously and this, along with the desire to feel more feminine, meant that many spent more time at hairdressers' salons than they had done before. As hair was such an important aspect of the appearance, it was recognised that hairdressers were doing a valuable job and many were exempt from war work in order to leave them available for perming, cutting and styling. Coiffured hair, make-up and jewellery became the main ways that women tried to enliven the look of their increasingly worn clothes and uniforms and to inject a little luxury into their lives.

A relatively recent invention of permanent waving using chemicals, heat and spiral curlers became extremely popular, replacing the previous, often dangerous and limiting method of being attached to a machine in the salon. This inevitably caused problems during the Blitz, so for many reasons, the chemical perm was welcomed. Although short hair would have been more practical, most women preferred the glamour of longer hair that they saw in Hollywood films, particularly the cascading waves of Veronica Lake. So during the day hair was pinned or tied off the face and kept out of the way of machinery with turbans, scarves, snoods, combs, grips or "bobby pins". Perms became almost essential to keep unruly hair in check, to ensure that the style adhered to the fashionable "not a hair out of place" look, while remaining bouncy, curly and controllable. Hairdressers, like everyone else, suffered with the shortages and it became a real problem for most to obtain their vital supplies of perm solution, bleach and most of all, shampoo. Various methods of making shampoo were developed. Some shredded cake soap and mixed it with boiling water, others dissolved a few Lux flakes – usually used for washing clothes – in water.

Many women made their own snoods, which began as a safety accessory and ended up as an essential fashion item of the war years. Many were knitted in different types and coloured yarns with beads attached to make wearers feel and look a little more glamorous. Snoods were not as hot to work in as turbans.

Coloured snood
This is an original knitting pattern for a snood:
1 oz wool, cotton or yarn
Pair knitting needles, size 0
Medium crochet hook
Round elastic to fit back of head
Cast on 42 stitches, first row knit, second row knit one*, (k 1, p 1, k 1) all in same stitch, purl three together from * to last stitch, knit one. Third row purl, fourth row knit one*, purl three together (k 1, p 1, k 1) all in same stitch, repeat from * to last stitch, knit one, fifth row purl. The last four rows form the pattern and are repeated until the work measures 14 inches (or suitable length). Cast off, but do not break off yarn. Make up – holding the elastic against the knitting, work double crochet over it into the edge of the knitting. Work round three sides, leaving the cast-off edge plain for front of head. Draw up the elastic to a suitable length and sew neatly to beginning and end of double crochet.

Women's magazines continued to appeal to their readers to remain resourceful and frequently gave recipes and ideas for simulating toiletries and cosmetics. For instance, bicarbonate of soda was dusted under the arms as an anti-perspirant, while Reckitt's Blue; a clothes whitening product, was used to brighten grey hair. Other ideas included:

- *To stop hair falling out, grind some dried parsley seeds and rub the powder into hair sparingly;*
- *To prevent wrinkles: collect rain water and add a handful of barley, boil the mixture and add it to a little white balsam to make a paste; apply it to the face once a day;*
- *To eliminate pimples, wet some saltpetre and dab it on the spots;*
- *To make hair grow quickly, crush a handful of nettles and stew them for a short time with a little water, then rub on to the scalp and comb hair in upward direction*

Simulated stockings

Some shops offered stocking-darning services, but more girls and women tried replicating the look of stocking seams down the backs of the legs with eyebrow pencil or the sooty end of a used match. This needed a steady hand (or a good friend who could do it for you). A pre-prepared stain for the legs could be bought from chemists or some women used gravy browning or onion skins to tint their legs, but as food was scarce for all, dogs or flies would usually follow them, which was quite off-putting! Another problem with that was if you were caught in the rain, your legs would become streaky. Tea was suggested as a suitable tint by some, but with only a few ounces allowed on ration each week, this was rarely taken up or if it was, the tea was so weak, having been used so many times to make cups of tea, that it was practically useless. Any methods of colouring the legs had to be washed off each night or the colour rubbed off on the sheets and most of the staining ingredients also stained the hands, which was difficult to remove with only a little soap – then again the whole process had to be repeated the following day. With all these difficulties, eventually most women moved on to either not wearing stockings at all or wearing socks.

Salvage

From the moment war broke out, the concept of salvaging was adopted by everyone on the Home Front with enthusiasm. The war effort demanded huge amounts of raw materials for uniforms, armaments, fuel and more and women, men and children were urged to play their part and save paper, rags, bottles and jars, bones, food waste and scrap metal. At the end of many streets large bins appeared, labelled for each type of salvage being collected: rags; food scraps to feed the pigs; tins and silver foil; scrap paper; bottles and jars and another for bones, which was made into fertiliser, glue or soap. As the bins were collected, the contents were sent to a network of collection depots. One campaign ran: "Every scrap of food stuff saved is a blow to Hitler's U-Boats which are out to starve us. Here is your chance to beat the enemy in your own kitchen. Put your reply to Hitler's threat in the waste food bin."

The campaign to collect scrap metal had been launched by

Chamberlain's government, but was propelled enthusiastically by Lord Beaverbrook and Lady Reading. Soon everyone was collecting any metal that they no longer used, including aluminium saucepans and other cooking utensils, coat hangers, toothpaste and shaving cream tubes (these toiletry containers were made of metal during the 1940s), paint pots, ornaments and even thimbles. By 1944 scrap metal was being saved at the rate of 110,000 tonnes per week. Whether the practical results of this exercise were as effective as people believed or not, the psychological results were huge.

In the eagerness to help the war effort through salvage, several terrible mistakes occurred while some were prevented just in time. Love letters and other, perhaps more valuable manuscripts, were sent to the pulping machine. Not only beautiful gates and railings, but also historically significant items were also scrapped, including weapons from significant events, such as cannons from the Spanish Armada of 1588 and the 1746 Battle of Culloden. Fortunately by August 1942 the government declared that antiquities were not to be used as salvage under any circumstances. As the war progressed, the need for salvage increased and people were exhorted to intensify their recycling. Government appeals (from the Ministry of Supply and the Ministry of Works) appeared in every newspaper and everyone threw themselves more fervently into this form of passive resistance. In February 1942 the *Picture Post* ran this poem:

> "The war is driving Hitler back
> And here's one way to win it,
> Just give your salvage men the sack
> And see there's plenty in it."

Almost everything could be salvaged, from envelopes to empty food cans, to rubber tyres. Paper was a popular commodity to salvage and approximately 50 million books were pulped over the course of the war. Six newspapers could be recycled into four boxes for rifle bullets. By the spring of 1943 there was enough kitchen waste being collected to feed 210,000 pigs every month; 130,000 tons of rubber had been reclaimed and 110,000 tons of scrap metal were being collected each week.

Threat of invasion

On 16th July 1940 Hitler had issued a statement: "As England, in spite of the hopelessness of her military position, has so far shown herself unwilling to come to any compromise, I have decided to begin to prepare for, and if necessary to carry out, an invasion…and if necessary the island will be occupied." So invasion by the Germans was a real fear for the British. As the surrounding sea and coastline was so intensely defended, it was predicted that enemy troops would land by parachute across the country. To this end signposts and station names were removed, while radio announcements warned listeners that the enemy would most probably be in disguise. From the start of the war, the Home Guard had been established, but an additional resistance force was planned to fight invaders. Men with detailed local knowledge were recruited from different areas and a handbook was prepared to explain methods of maiming, incapacitating and killing, along with the locations of secret refuges where they could hide and lie low if necessary. Beaches were off limits as barbed wire and heavy artillery lined the coastline. It was suggested that German spies could be among the people at any time; suspicions were roused and to prevent any secrets being spilled, posters everywhere warned: "Careless Talk Costs Lives", "Keep It Under Your Hat, You Never Know Who's Listening", "Keep Mum, She's Not So Dumb" and "Tell Nobody, Not Even Her!" (These last two were implying that even an attractive female date could potentially be a spy.) This propaganda was a huge success because it was simple to understand and it made everyone laugh. Pat Parsons remembered:

"Although having spies and German invaders among us without our knowing was a threat, I don't remember the idea making us any more worried than we had been already. I sometimes sat on the bus or stood in queues with my mum and tried to work out if the person next to me might be a spy. I suppose we were just all so confidant we would win the war, the thought of enemies among us just didn't seem real!"

National Savings

Shortages, salvage and threats to security were common and overriding themes on the Home Front for the duration of the war. With so many materials and components needed for armaments, uniforms and civilian use, shortages and salvage were unrelenting. The one thing that was improving, however, was the ability of the public to earn money. Before the war there had been just under four million income tax payers in Britain, but by 1941, there were six million and by 1945, 12,500,000 Britons paid income tax. Pay as you earn was another wartime innovation, introduced in 1940 to make paying income tax easier for weekly wage earners.

Although income tax rose to seven shillings and sixpence in the pound in 1939 and to 10 shillings in the pound by 1941, with purchase tax on luxury goods rising to 100 per cent, taxation did not meet the financial needs of the war. National Savings had been introduced during World War One to help the government's funding and in November 1939, a new campaign was launched by the Chancellor of the Exchequer with the slogan: "Lend to Defend the Right to be Free". National Savings worked by persuading people to buy National Savings Stamps at sixpence or two shillings and sixpence each. When anyone had saved a total of 15 shillings worth of stamps, they could exchange the stamps for a National Savings Certificate or for £5 they could buy a Defence Bond. Both National Savings Certificates and Defence Bonds were guaranteed to give a return after the war. Defence Bonds offered a return of three per cent and a small tax-free bonus on maturity. As well as certificates and bonds, there were also local collections to raise money for aeroplanes, tanks, weapons and any items which were urgently needed. Volunteers, especially members of the WVS, organised the Local Savings Committees, which in turn, were supported by national committees. The idea of saving to help the war effort was already established and the National Savings movement was a great success. Many people bought a weekly sixpenny savings stamp and National Savings Certificates became frequent and acceptable wartime gifts between close friends and relatives or even as school prizes. The advertising made it easy for people to save regularly as not only was everyone else doing it, but it was seen as being highly patriotic; and

When the war began, most people thought it would be over in a matter of weeks. Audrey O'Connell was as positive as everyone else.

The War Emergency Information and Instructions leaflet was issued early on to help civilians feel safer and that they were not alone in the fight.

WAR EMERGENCY

INFORMATION AND
INSTRUCTIONS

Read this leaflet carefully and make sure that you and all other responsible persons in your house understand its contents.

Pay no attention to rumours. Official news will be given in the papers and over the wireless.

Listen carefully to all broadcast instructions and be ready to note them down.

8

(14) NATIONAL HEALTH INSURANCE.

If you are insured under National Health Insurance you should, if you leave home, take with you your current contribution card and your medical card.

If you require medical attention in the place to which you go, you will be able to get it from an insurance doctor there. If you need sickness, disablement or maternity benefit, you should write to your Approved Society or go to their local agent.

(15) GENERAL INSTRUCTIONS.

Carry your gas mask with you always.

Do not allow your children to run about the streets.

Avoid waste of any kind whether of food, water, electricity or gas.

Obey promptly any instructions given you by the police, the special constables, the air raid wardens, or any other authorised persons and be ready to give them any assistance for which they ask you.

DO NOT TAKE TOO MUCH NOTICE OF NOISE IN AN AIR RAID. MUCH OF IT WILL BE THE NOISE OF OUR OWN GUNS DEALING WITH THE RAIDERS.

KEEP A GOOD HEART: WE ARE GOING TO WIN THROUGH.

51-4383 2

Propaganda boosted morale and instructed the public on how they could help the war effort. By 1941 when this leaflet was issued, anyone who *didn't* save and salvage was frowned upon or even fined.

This photo of children wearing gas masks shows them looking quite happy, but most found the rubber smell overpowering, with the whole experience of wearing them claustrophobic and frightening.

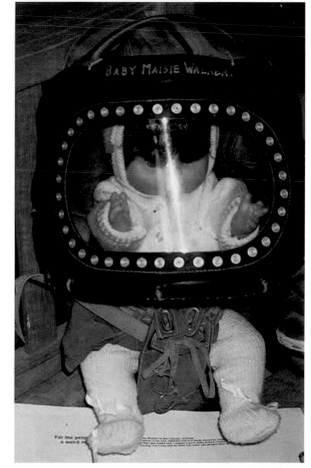

BABY MAISIE WALKER.

A doll in a baby's gas mask; gas masks for babies were issued along with all the other masks. Conscientious mothers learned to put them on their infants in a matter of seconds.

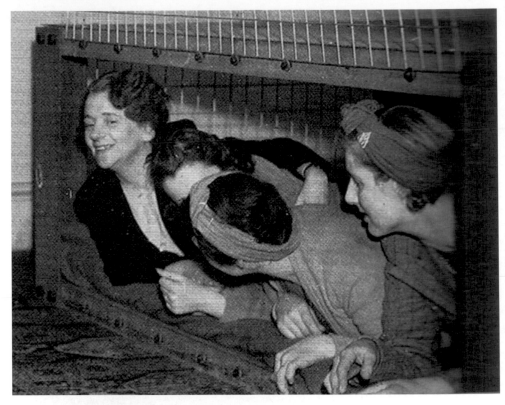

Inside a Morrison shelter. Many city households had Morrison shelters which were used as tables during the day.

Everyone had to carry their gas masks at all times and to know how to use them.

Calling all women! Audrey O'Connell in her ATS uniform.

Women took on many traditionally masculine roles and undertook tasks that formerly had been restricted to the realm of men.

The chain of buckets to extinguish a fire symbolises the chain of resourcefulness and solidarity among women at home for the duration of the war.

The WVS was made up of women from all social backgrounds and they worked tirelessly to maintain some form of normality. For instance, they undertook the bulk of the evacuation programme.

The Women's Land Army prevented Britain from being starved into submission. It was strenuous work and not as glamorous as it was portrayed in the advertising.

With their stalwart and positive attitudes, women really did 'keep the home fires burning' for the men fighting at the Front.

Vegetable Marrow and Tomato

Peel marrow—remove seeds—cut in slices—parboil then sauté in hot fat until tender—peel and slice a few tomatoes—arrange on baking dish alternately with sliced marrow, and when the dish is full, season, and, if liked, sprinkle the top with grated cheese or browned crumbs. Baste with gravy, and bake in a hot oven for a few minutes.

Potato Short Bread

3 ozs. margarine	4 ozs. warm mashed potato
2 ozs. rice flour	3 ozs. flour
A pinch of salt	2 ozs. sugar
A little almond flavouring	

Cream fat and sugar, then add mashed potato, beat well, then rice flour, salt and flavouring. Take out spoon and with hands lightly press the flour (containing a little baking powder) into the mixture—roll out and bake.

Potato Cheese

Line patty-tins with pastry.
Mixture :

2 ozs. fat creamed with	Almond flavouring
2 ozs. sugar	1 oz. cornflour
2 dried eggs or 1 fresh egg	2 ozs. apples, minced and fried
¼ lb. potato pulp	slightly in a little hot fat
½ pint milk	

Make milk and cornflour into a sauce, work in the eggs, creamed fat and sugar and potato. Put a little jam in bottom of pastry, put mixture on top. If liked, apples may be peeled, cored, cut into sections and placed overlapping on top. Bake about twenty minutes.

Potato Suet Paste

½ lb. flour—put into a bowl	¾ teaspoonful baking powder
4 ozs. chopped suet	½ teaspoonful salt

Mix well, add ½ lb. warm mashed potato, mix lightly. When thoroughly mixed squeeze together to form a paste, probably without using any moisture. May be used for potato pie.

Potato Pie

Mixture : Fry 1 oz. onion, fat, and a sprinkle of flour together, add ½ pint of water or stock, 3 ozs. cooked meat, trimmings from bones, etc., ½ teaspoonful mixed herbs, put into pan and cook together for a few minutes, then add ½ lb. potato cut up (cooked or uncooked), a little more water if necessary, season nicely.

Roll out half the paste, cut in two strips, line sides of dish—none at bottom—trim and decorate edges of pastry, put mixture in dish, decorate top with slices of partially cooked potato overlapping, put a little dripping on top. Bake about thirty minutes.

Potato Macaroni Pudding

In a bowl put :

½ lb. mashed potatoes	A little chopped parsley
2 ozs. nuts, chopped	2 ozs. suet
1 oz. fried onion	1 egg
A pinch of mixed herbs,	4 ozs. flour, containing ½ tea-
pepper, salt and nutmeg	spoonful baking powder
1 oz. cooked chopped macaroni	

Mix very well together, do not make too moist, put into greased basin, steam for one-and-a-half to two hours. Serve with brown gravy sauce.

Onion and Cheese Pudding

1 large sliced onion	1 oz. flour
1 oz. fat	

Fry onion. Move to one side, and fry flour. Add 1½ pints water, seasoning, and simmer till onion is tender. Sprinkle strips of bread with grated cheese. Place in layers in greased pie-dish, pour the soup over, and bake until brown.

Recipes were issued in leaflets, in magazines and on posters. There were seemingly endless ways of cooking appetising meals without the staple ingredients that everyone had been used to.

Women's Land Army recruits turned the empty fields of Britain into fertile and productive farmlands, ensuring that the population could eat healthily when most other supplies had been cut off.

The leaflet, 'Your Children's Food in Wartime' advised on health and nutrition for hard-pressed mothers.

'Dig for Victory Now' was one of the most successful campaigns of the war.

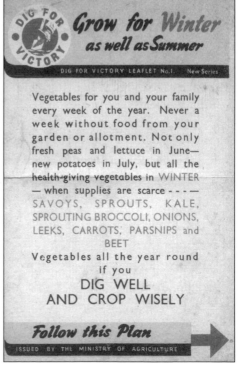

Picking fruit became a popular summer pastime when queues were long and shops' produce reduced.

War On Disease

THE Germans taught us a valuable lesson—that the appeasement of a warmonger is useless. This lesson must determine our attitude to disease. Only a very strong defensive system will discourage those persistent warmongers—the germs—which cause half a million fatal casualties in our civilian ranks every year. It is high time, too, that we developed an effective counter-attack.

This leaflet will tell you something about the enemy—about

INFECTIOUS DISEASES

AND HOW THEY SPREAD

AND HOW THEY CAN BE AVOIDED AND PREVENTED

KNOW YOUR ENEMY

Infectious diseases are caused by germs. They thrive best in the human body, but many of them can live, for a time at least, in the air or on handkerchiefs, cups, etc. Fresh air, sunlight and soap and water are the enemies of germs; gloom, dust, and crowded stuffy rooms are their friends. Strong heat kills germs. If an article is boiled any germs on it will be killed.

COUGHS AND SNEEZES SPREAD DISEASES

Germs which cause coughs and colds are spread by the breath—shot out into the air during speaking, but still more during coughing or sneezing. The most important diseases spread in this way are the infectious diseases of children—like measles, diphtheria, whooping cough, scarlet fever, chicken-pox, mumps and German measles. But there are others which affect adults too—like consumption (tuberculosis), influenza, colds and tonsillitis. And there are also certain rarer but very serious diseases—like spotted fever (cerebro-spinal meningitis) and infantile paralysis.

We can all help to lessen the spread of these diseases. We should cover our mouth with a handkerchief when coughing and sneezing. We should avoid over-crowded, stuffy rooms as much as possible. If we catch an infectious disease we should keep away from other people whenever possible—and we should not spit. We can, and should, protect our children against diphtheria by having them immunized—by small injections into the skin. These are almost painless and quite harmless. All wise parents will have their children done as soon as they are a year old. The people at the Public Health Department at the Town Hall or Council Offices will tell you how to get this treatment. It is free.

One way in which we can lessen the danger of passing on any germs we may have in our mouth is by avoiding the habit of licking our fingers before turning pages, counting money and opening paper bags.

HOW THEY START

Many infectious diseases start with symptoms very like those of a cold and it is often difficult, even for a doctor, to tell at first whether a person (usually a child) has a cold or a more serious infection. It is safer, therefore, to consult a doctor about a child's cold—especially if there are any of these symptoms:

The threat of disease and illness was a great fear at home during the war. By growing your own food, it was hoped that individuals could take responsibility for themselves and keep themselves healthy.

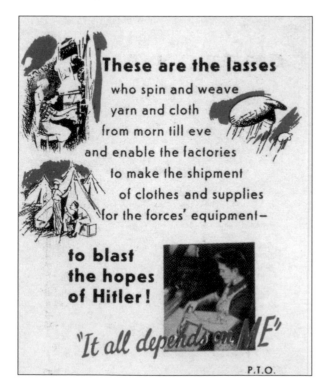

Advertising encouraged women who found themselves working in strange jobs for long hours, imparting the feeling that they were making a positive impact on the war.

'It all depends on ME' was another clever piece of propaganda – it also promoted the notion that women could continue to be beautiful while undertaking jobs that had previously only been done by men.

This campaign told women everywhere in Britain that they were personally making a positive difference in the fight against Hitler.

P.T.O.

As a symbol of femininity, stockings were a problem. Despite the best efforts of knitting companies and magazines however, woolly knitted versions never really caught on!

Snoods were chic and stylish ways of keeping hair neat when working with machinery.

Mr and Mrs Sutton on their wedding day in 1941; proof that even in wartime, brides could be beautiful.

Audrey O'Connell in her timeless home-made coat.

In order to keep stylish, many women became particularly accomplished at knitting.

Along with socks and balaclavas for soldiers, many people knitted scarves for themselves and their families. As the leaflets said: women had to be their own clothes' 'doctors'.

Little silver beads give this scarf its sparkle. They are actually knitted into the fabric, but that doesn't make the knitting difficult or tedious. Try it; the pretty effect is well worth the little extra trouble.

Knitting and sewing patterns were in abundance as everyone aimed to be as enterprising as possible. Keeping up appearances generated a positive feeling.

Style and Simplicity

A "STOCKING" CAP, AND GLOVES TO MATCH

MATERIALS
5 oz. 3-ply wool.
4 No. 13 needles with points at both ends.

MEASUREMENTS
Cap length, 19 ins.
Gloves to fit average hand.

TENSION
8 sts. to 1 in.

CAP
Cast on 150 sts. (50 on each of 3 needles). Work in moss st. thus:—
1st round.—* K. 1, p. 1 rep. from * to end.
2nd round.—* P. 1, k. 1, rep. from * to end.
Rep. these 2 rounds until work measures 19 ins. Cast off.

THE GLOVES
The Left Hand.—Cast on 60 sts. (20 on each of 3 needles).
Work in moss st. as given for cap for 2½ ins., finish end of round.
Shape Thumb thus:—
1st round.—Moss st. 27, inc. twice in next st. thus. K. into right half of next st. in previous row, then work the st. itself, then work into left half of the same st. in previous row, moss st. 32.
Work 3 rounds without shaping after each inc. round.
5th round.—Moss st. 28, inc. twice in next st., moss st. 33.
9th round.—Moss st. 29, inc. twice in next st., moss st. 34.

13th round.—Moss st. 30 inc. twice in next st., moss st. 35.
17th round.—Moss st. 31, inc. twice in next st., moss st. 36.
21st round.—Moss st. 32, inc. twice in next st., moss st. 37
25th round.—Moss st. 33, inc. twice in next st., moss st. 38.
26th round.—Moss st. 27, sl. the next 15 thumb sts. on to length of wool, cast on 3 sts., moss st. to end.
27th round.—Moss st. 27, take 3 tog., moss st. to end (60 sts.).
Work 1½ ins. on these sts., finish end of round.

A second suggestion for wearing your hat.

K.B.6—C   Page 65

Even with the clothing restrictions there was room for some individual creativity.

A simple two-colour pattern worked in dark red and grey, was used for the matching scarf and gloves. The same instructions can, of course, be adapted to a plain set, but the gay colour scheme would please most men.

Scarves were often made from wool unpicked from old jumpers; nothing went to waste.

Workers became accustomed to listening to the wireless as they worked, which helped to keep everyone cheerful.

A bombed-out family in London being resolute and courageous. This was a common sight in city streets.

Children being evacuated was another familiar sight. Hundreds of little children, labelled and carrying suitcases, were sent off to distant places, supposedly to be safer than in the cities.

Going into an Anderson shelter in a back garden. During the day, these were snug and many families decorated theirs, but at night they were dank and dark, and most were soon abandoned.

Waiting for a train to evacuate them, these children took their parents' lead and on the whole, remained cheerful, despite the bewilderment and fear many felt.

Maisie Walker clearly remembers the day she said goodbye to her beloved brother.

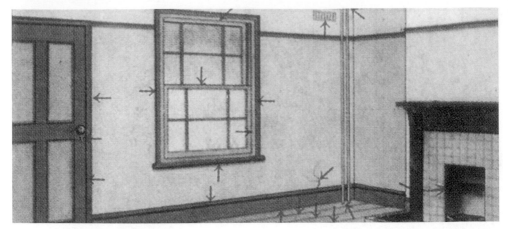

There was a real fear of being gassed during the early part of the war, so plenty of information was issued on how to render the home gas-proof.

Not many people had homes big enough for this, but one idea promoted by the government was to prepare a refuge room in case of emergency. Most people with houses used their under stair cupboards.

Air raid wardens patrolled the streets of vulnerable areas. Although they were necessarily strict about the blackout, they were also reassuring, friendly and reliable.

Natural optimism spurred on the British at this time, and this became the greatest national symbol of hope; St Paul's Cathedral still standing when all around was devastated by bombs.

The numerous, depressing elements of the war were not dwelt on; there was an unspoken code of responsibility to keep smiling and pretend that all was well. In the main, it worked!

Hose laying lorries were a common sight, as were groups of volunteers who had been trained by charities or the local council to do this work or to work as ambulance crew.

Sir Winston Churchill instilled confidence and offered encouragement. He just had to turn up to wave the troops off to give everyone a positive mental boost.

Audrey O'Connell's release book from the ATS, received at the end of the war.

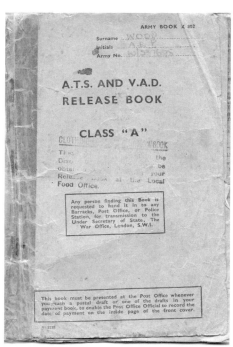

At the end of the war women had to give up the jobs they had learned to do so quickly and so well. It was another adjustment they faced with fortitude and determination.

Even after the war ended in Europe, most members of the armed forces had to carry on until Victory in Japan was declared in August.

When the war ended, there remained the massive problem of rebuilding Britain's devastated cities.

after the war everyone would be reimbursed with profit. It was a win-win situation, with favourable outcomes guaranteed. From 1940 and for the entirety of the war, local Savings Weeks became a regular aspect of daily life. Related themed weeks occurred constantly, for instance, "War Weapons Weeks" were held from September 1940 to October 1941, followed by "Warship Weeks" from October 1941 to March 1942 and "Wings for Victory Weeks" from early in 1943 until the following autumn. With the focus on different needs the public could see that their savings were needed constantly to help different branches of the armed forces and different aspects of the war and so no one became indifferent or complacent. Running a savings group appealed to many who could not participate more actively in the war. These people collected money, sorted out the paperwork and generally made sure that the system worked – and all voluntarily. Endorsing the patriotic feel, advertising slogans declared: "Back them up with war savings" ['them' being the men away fighting] or "Fight in the streets; belong to your savings group" [implying that you could help to win the war by saving]. Then of course, there was the Squander Bug that was invented specifically to promote the National Savings movement and to crush the urge to spend.

Furniture and homes

During the war, there were fewer home owners in Britain than there are now, which made it easier to move about; which was just as well as there were 60 million changes of address over the six years. By 1941 over two million homes were destroyed by bombing, which accounted for some of the movement, while some was through evacuation and some because of war work. While homes were less permanent, furniture was more enduring. Heavy, well made and relatively expensive, it was considered to be a twice in a lifetime purchase, usually bought by newly weds on Hire Purchase (fondly termed the 'never-never'). But as the war progressed, there was a huge shortage of furniture with an acute timber deficiency. In November 1942 the Board of Trade banned the manufacture of any furniture except 22 indispensable items and initiated the Utility Furniture Scheme. Utility furniture was made to standardised specifications that were functional rather than decorative following

Board of Trade specifications that had tight controls on the amount and quality of materials to be used for making the furniture. Not everyone could buy it though. Utility furniture could be bought by newly weds, those who had been bombed out of their homes, and certain others. A docket to purchase it was required and even then, allowances were restricted. The furniture was valued by units and individuals were allocated certain amounts. For instance, a wardrobe was 12 units and an armchair six. A couple was allowed 60 units between them; a child was allowed 10 units. The furniture still had to be paid for, but the Central Price Regulation Committee (the CPRC) set strict price controls for it all and for second-hand furniture. Although basic and simple, all utility furniture was solidly made and every item had the CC41 utility mark etched on it. This logo was taken from the utility clothing scheme, which had been launched earlier and stood for "Civilian Clothing 1941".

Utility furniture was designed by an Advisory Committee that included some of the best designers in the country, including the respected designer and writer on furniture, John Gloag; the chairman of the largest furniture manufacturer in the world, Herman Lebus; and the furniture designer and craftsman Gordon Russell. The committee aimed to ensure the production of strong, well-designed furniture that took into account the scarcity of timber and other materials and was reasonably priced. Following the traditions of the Arts and Crafts movement, the designs were made of good quality materials and were devoid of superfluous ornament. About 700 furniture manufacturers around the country produced utility furniture, which led to unavoidable variations in quality. In 1943 the Advisory Committee produced the Utility Furniture Catalogue, which featured the utility designs in five sections, including: living room; bedroom; kitchen; nursery furniture and a final section that included miscellaneous items, such as a sofa-bed and a bookcase.

All utility furniture was usually made of strong, serviceable British wood, such as oak, with mortise and tendon joints, or dowelling and glue. First made in England in 1898 by hot pressing waste paper, hardboard came into its own during the war and was also used, veneered, in some of the furniture. Handles and knobs were made of wood rather than metal, as metal was vital for other things, although some metal screws were used in parts, such as hinges, which added greatly to the strength of the furniture.

Household repairs
In December 1940, the Ministry of Home Security issued a leaflet: *After the Raid*, giving advice for those whose homes had been hit by bombs or had suffered related damage. As helpful and clear as ever, it included information on "Compensation for Damage to Houses":

> "If you own your own house or hold it on a long lease and it is damaged or destroyed, whatever your income, you should, as soon as possible, make a claim on Form VOW1 [you can get this form at your Town Hall or the offices of your Council]. The amount of your compensation and the time of paying it will depend on the passing of the War Damage Bill now before Parliament."

There was also advice on how you could be helped by the authorities with simple repairs:

> "If your house can be made fit to live in with a few simple repairs the local authority (apply to the Borough or Council Engineer) will put it right if the landlord is not able to do it. But how quickly the local authority can do this depends on local conditions."

But as ever during the war everyone was also encouraged to help themselves and carry out their own repairs wherever possible. *The Daily Express* book *Wartime Household Repairs* stated: "Most of the houses which suffer as a result of raids are made uncomfortable rather than dangerous and if you are by nature a handy person, you will want to set about making the place once more habitable." It was estimated that between 33 per cent and 20 per cent of all homes in Britain were damaged as a direct result of bombing – even if this was just shattered windows, cracked chimney stacks or missing roof tiles. Materials and skilled craftsmen were scarce, so the only option was to do things for yourself. "Make Do and Mend" was a variation of a pre-war phrase "Make and Mend" used in the 1939 *News Chronicle* DIY book, *Modern Make and Mend*. When the phrase make do and mend was launched it covered every aspect of everyday life, with ordinary householders being urged to repair or make things themselves and so saving the meagre resources of materials and manpower. Like several other household books of the time, *Modern Make and Mend*, dealt with most of the standard wartime themes in terms of minor house repairs, such as cracks in ceilings or vacuum cleaner repairs, but it also gave tips and advice on building new items, mending shoes, pressing clothes and safe air raid precautions in the home. Another feature in the book was on making gifts for Christmas and birthdays, and generally books and magazine articles like these encouraged people to think creatively and practically and to be innovative with what little they had to improve things around them.

The idea of taking responsibility for oneself was extremely important during the war. It was dispensed quite delicately with a balance of support from the government and all the appropriate ministries, so that the public felt protected, but also accountable for themselves and each other. This approach promoted a sense of self-worth as well as camaraderie – the idea that people were independent, while still being protected and cared for. Through leaflets, editorial and advertising, the information and advice kept on coming. Enforcing this idea, at the bottom of the *After the Raid* leaflet, was the message:

> "Keep this and do what it tells you. Help is waiting for you. The government, your fellow citizens and your neighbours will see that 'Front Line' fighters are looked after!"

The Battle for Fuel
In 1942 the Ministry of Fuel and Power issued a leaflet entitled 'Here are your battle orders', which began:

> "Every citizen – particularly every housewife – is now in the Front Line in the vital Battle for Fuel. Everything possible must be done to save fuel."

It went on to give practical hints for saving fuel at home. Extremely informative, it explained about reading gas and electricity meters, allowances, units and also giving numerous practical tips about saving fuel in the house.

Among the many shortages in Britain during the war, fuel was probably the least expected. In 1940, when the occupation of France meant that overseas sales fell drastically, Britain had too much coal. In consequence, mining ceased to be a reserved occupation and thousands of miners aged 30 or under were called up or volunteered for the armed forces. Then, by the following year, the reverse had happened. Coal was suddenly in radically short supply. In panic, miners were recalled from the army. But still, with fewer workers than before, the coal-mining industry had been depleted and output remained low. By January 1942 the government began appealing to the public to save fuel. Petrol had been rationed since the start of the war and rationing of fuel was discussed extensively, but the logistics would have been too complicated, so in the end, householders were asked to "do their bit"; to remove light bulbs that were not essential, to eat cold food whenever possible and to reduce their washing – of clothes, dishes and themselves. Everyone made the effort by:

- saving washing-up and laundry to do in one large go
- sitting together in one room with only one fire
- sitting with friends one or two nights a week so only one fire is used
- using only one bar of an electric heater or keeping a gas fire on low
- using the smallest gas ring when cooking
- sprinkling soda crystals (for washing clothes) on coal to make it burn less quickly
- bathing only once a week or sharing bath water
- keeping warm by walking up and down stairs, layering clothes or going to bed early
- only using the iron for several items at once: "Iron a lot while the iron's hot"
- tacking strips of felt around draughty doors and windows
- only filling the kettle with the right amount of water needed

• turning off lights as they left a room and only having low wattage light bulbs in areas not used much, such as halls and passageways.

The government introduced the idea of everyone being restricted to just one weekly bath and only using a small amount of water. The expression "The Battle for Fuel" came to be used for all energy conservation. By 1942 a notice was issued to all hotels and guest houses that read: "As part of your personal share in the Battle for Fuel you are asked NOT to exceed five inches of water in this bath. Make it a point of honour not to fill the bath above this level." Outside posters for rail companies reminded everyone that: "At this most important time, needless travel is a crime", while posters for the Ministry of Fuel and Power announced: "Britain's 12,000,000 households are 12,000,000 battle fronts in this great drive to save fuel". As with many other wartime campaigns the public responded well, dramatically cutting waste. From 1938 to 1945 British coal use was reduced by 25 per cent. In 1943 the Ministry of Food issued *War Cookery leaflet no. 9* "Fuel Saving in the Kitchen". It began:

"We must save fuel of every kind, whether it be coal, coke, gas, electricity, oil or paraffin. The war industries must have all they need and every pennyworth of fuel saved in the home means more for the factory or the shipyards."

The leaflet continued by telling readers never to overcook food, to keep saucepans, kettles and other cooking utensils scrupulously clean but not to polish the bottom of pans as "a clean dull surface absorbs heat more rapidly than a shiny one". Further ideas for energy saving were passed around families, such as:

"Everyone turned lights off that were not absolutely necessary."

"When my mum finished cooking, she opened the oven door and we used the heat to warm the room – everyone sat in the kitchen rather than the living room."

In the book *101 Things to Do in Wartime* of 1940 it was suggested that low-wattage lamps should be fitted with reflector shades to increase the light. This could be achieved by painting the inside of a shade with white paint or making a white paper lining. In 1944 the Ministry of Fuel and Power advertised "Is YOUR home helping to build a destroyer? Save fuel for battle." The copy declared: "5lbs of coal saved in one day by 1,500,000 homes will provide enough fuel to build a destroyer." The small print explained: "5lbs of coal are used in two hours by a gas fire or electric oven."

If ever there was a reason to conserve fuel, that was it.

6
THE CLOTHES DOCTOR

"If every single garment in the homes of Britain, every pot and pan, every sheet, every towel is used and kept usable until not even a magician could hold it together any longer, the war will be won more surely and quickly." ~ Hugh Dalton, President of the Board of Trade, in 1942

From early on in the war, clothes, household linens and soft furnishings became difficult to obtain as fabrics imports were discontinued and many factories that had produced civilian clothes began making uniforms and other war equipment. Consequently prices for clothes and other fabric products soared and, in June 1941, clothes rationing was introduced. Although the shortages and high costs were problems, the overriding reason for clothes rationing was to release some of the 450,000 people employed in the clothing industry for other, more vital war work. Oliver Lyttelton, who was President of the Board of Trade from 1940-41 and in 1945, announced the launch of clothes rationing on the radio, saying: "In war the term 'battle-stained' is an honourable one. We must learn as civilians to be seen in clothes that are not so smart…because we are bearing yet another share of the war. When you are tired of your old clothes, remember that by making them do you are contributing some part of an aeroplane, a gun or a tank." Two years later, Hugh Dalton, the next President of the Board of Trade (from 1942-45) told the nation: "The people of this country can congratulate themselves…in the first twelve months, more than a quarter of a million tons of shipping were saved in textiles alone. Nearly four hundred thousand men and women have been released from making cloth and clothing for civilians and have gone into the Services or to war production."

"Make Do and Mend" was adopted at the same time as clothes rationing as a slogan by the government to encourage everyone to repair and reuse their old clothes. Second-hand clothes were not rationed and clothing was handed down through families, sold on or swapped. Adults were allowed a fixed number of clothing coupons per year, each item of clothing having a coupon value, plus the price fixed by the Central Price Regulation Committee. Clothing ration books were pink and initially every adult was given 66 coupons a year, dropping to 48 in 1942 and 36 in 1943. With a man's coat costing 16 coupons, a woman's 14 and a child's 11 it is clear how difficult things became. An adult's cardigan took eight coupons, or five for a child, while a man's suit was 26 coupons. A complete outfit with underwear could use up a person's entire clothing allocation for the year. An extra allowance of 50 coupons was given to expectant mothers but, even so, things were still extremely difficult and the regulations were quite complex. In August 1941, the Board of Trade issued the "Clothing Coupon Quiz", to clarify issues surrounding clothes rationing. It began:

> "There is enough for all if we share and share alike. Rationing is the way to get fair shares. *Fair shares* – when workers are producing guns, aeroplanes and bombs instead of frocks, suits and shoes. *Fair shares* – when ships must run the gauntlet with munitions and food rather than with wool and cotton. *Fair shares* – when movements of population outrun local supplies. It is your scheme – to defend you as a consumer and as a citizen. All honest people realise that trying to beat the ration is the same as trying to cheat the nation."

The "Clothing Coupon Quiz" included 100 questions and answers, explaining clothes rationing clearly and straightforwardly, but given the many occupations of people in Britain at the time and differing scenarios that could occur, it was rather complicated. For example, how to buy clothing for children who were evacuated, how to buy clothes for others and whether or not there would be any extra allowances for special occasions, such as weddings? (The answer to the last question was no.) Anyone could buy anyone else's clothes for them using their coupons and as can be imagined, clothing coupons became a valuable commodity to barter with – for some. The "Clothing Coupon Quiz" explained how those who had been bombed out of their homes could obtain replacement coupons (if people's clothes were destroyed by bombing, they could apply for up to two years' worth of coupons); how essential items of clothing could be obtained for those who worked for services such as nursing or the police; or how items that were not on the government's list would be valued in terms of coupons. It pointed out that school uniforms had to come out of clothing rations. In reality, this meant that many families had to pool their coupons in order to buy the necessary items, including blazers, shorts, blouses or shirts and so on.

When clothes rationing began, 26 of the allocated 66 coupons were actually margarine coupons that were already in use, which caused some confusion. Later on, specific clothing coupons were printed (on recycled paper) and issued. Unlike food, clothing coupons could be redeemed at any shop or number of shops. They could be used at any rate and at any time. They could also be sent off for mail order clothing. Some uniforms were not rationed, while some, such as those for nurses or the police were, as were knitting yarns and dress fabrics, for instance. Inevitably, an illegal black market developed with unscrupulous traders selling the unobtainable, but at a price. Further illicit trading occurred with people selling counterfeit coupons, until the government issued new rules making any previously detached coupons invalid (except when used for mail order). Coupons had to be stamped in the book and detached by the shopkeeper at the point of sale. Another problem was that about 700,000 clothes ration books were lost or stolen in the early part of the scheme. When somebody died, the family was meant to return the deceased person's unused clothing rations, but this rarely happened as so precious were the coupons. Apart from all this, many of the country's families were simply too poor to buy any new clothes, even with coupons and at the regulated, government-fixed prices. So the make do and mend culture grew, and it became the norm to swap, sell or adapt old clothes; dyeing, unpicking, darning or sewing in efforts to look neat and to maintain self-confidence.

Be a magician

"No material must lie idle, so be a magician and turn old clothes into new" was a line in one of many Board of Trade leaflets dealing with the "Make Do and Mend" campaign. The leaflets encouraged creative enterprise as did the classes the government organised to show women how they could care for their clothes, make them last and renovate or remake them. *Make Do and Mend leaflet No. 8* was entitled "Every Woman her own Clothes Doctor". It began: "Here are a few treatments for a few common clothes complaints – all quite easy to carry out and all well worth doing." There followed tips on lengthening a dress; giving an old coat a fresh start; repairing pleats; making a decorative elbow patch; renewing worn gloves; replacing pockets and "keeping pace with a growing girl", among several other practical ideas. Other booklets discussed caring for woollens, how to patch a shirt, make buttonholes, darn or make clothes out of nylon, for instance. Scarves, bindings and ribbons were hoarded as they were useful for remodelling old clothes. If an item of clothing could not be mended or turned into something useful, it was unpicked or unravelled, added to other materials and turned into something completely new. Vivien Coulsdon recalled making necessary objects from papier-maché:

> "I made all sorts of things in the war, but some of my most successful 'creations' were papier-maché buckles. I tore up bits of newspaper and made a paste with flour and water. The paper pulp was quite malleable and I shaped it to make the buckle, adding a bit of bent wire to the central 'line'. When it was completely dry, I painted the buckle, not the wire, and then decorated it, with small painted flowers. I seem to remember using clear nail varnish to protect the whole thing. It was so successful that all my friends wanted one! So I made several as gifts and we attached them to home-made cloth belts."

Barbara Matthews remembers making hats for a wartime wedding:

"We plaited straw into thin plaits and then sewed them together in spiral hat shapes. Then we varnished them and made bows or flowers to sew on to them. It was a lot of difficult work!"

Jackie Watson recalled women turning their husbands' trousers into skirts for themselves. Trousers were easily converted into skirts or into boys' shorts by cutting off the bottom of the legs and unpicking the inner seams. Two triangular-shaped pieces of fabric cut from the legs were stitched into the space at the front and back and the entire garment was hemmed. An advertisement from the Board of Trade declared: "Nowadays every remade garment becomes a uniform of honour and every darn a 'decoration'." It went on to suggest that enough material could be salvaged from a man's shirt to make a school blouse for a small girl, or a pair of man's flannel trousers could provide enough fabric for a "warm little frock", using the top part for the bodice and a skirt from the leg portions.

Women did a lot of knitting before the war, but once it started, the skill came into its own. Posters announced such things as: "Our Jungle Fighters want Socks – Please Knit Now". So most evenings during the blackout, women and girls would listen to the radio and knit essential items such as jumpers, socks, mittens, scarves and balaclavas for the troops, for their families and for themselves. Girls were taught to knit from an early age, but in such a sexist era, boys were not. Maisie Walker remembers:

"Young girls were taught to knit on four needles at school to make balaclavas and mittens for the Forces and when at home, they unravelled old jumpers to knit into different garments for everyday wear. They were also taught how to do French Knitting, otherwise known as Knitting Nancy, and boys too learnt how to do this."

Women's magazines printed knitting patterns and hints and tips on how to care for garments or make an old outfit more fashionable.

Ideas included making dresses and skirts from blackout fabric, unravelling jumpers and using the wool to create new outfits, darning or patching clothes or making a skirt out of an old pair of trousers. Fair Isle became fashionable because it was made of small amounts of coloured yarn, which worked well when using up odd bits and pieces. In 1943, in an article entitled "Warmed up for winter", *Good Housekeeping* declared: "Here are some simple home recipes that add warmth and variety to a wilting wardrobe." It suggested:

"Take one or more tired frocks and spice them up with a cheerful sleeveless pullover made from the brightest scraps of woollen in your piece-box. Cut strips, join them by machine in the gayest colour combination you can manage, then cut out your pullover from this length of material. Line with oddments of strong cotton or woollen for firmness and extra warmth."

Sewing classes and advice centres where capable sewers and knitters taught others or advised on the best way to renovate clothes sprang up in church halls and local schools and women were encouraged to have "sewing parties", pooling their resources and ideas and generally helping each other.

Standard sizing

At such a time of shortages, the best possible use had to be made of scarce materials and so, in May 1940, the Distributive Industry (Standards) Committee started operating. The new committee's first task was the question of clothes sizing as a measure of economy, to reduce any wastage. The committee had to determine and create set sizes for a wide range of women's and children's clothing. Before the war and for years afterwards, women had complained about the diversity and confusion of clothes' sizing systems. The committee established a certain form of standard sizes during the war (this had already been achieved in uniforms for servicemen and women) but it was not until several years after the war that an agreed system was formed.

In 1943, the Board of Trade printed an article in *Good Housekeeping* on taking care of clothes. At the bottom of the article was a paragraph entitled "Count your Coupons". It began:

"When you are thinking of buying some garment or piece of material, count over your coupons and think of the warm things that you will need in the winter time. The cold weather is only a few weeks ahead. Better hold your coupons. Perhaps you can 'make do' for the present with the clothes you have."

The aim of the Board of Trade was to help rather than lay down the law. The intention was to maintain good humour, while helping everyone to feel independent and in control of their own lives as much as was possible. With that in mind, many "Make Do and Mend" booklets were issued, including one in 1943 with a foreword by Hugh Dalton, which began:

"First, I would like to thank you all for the way in which you have accepted clothes rationing. You know how it has saved much-needed shipping space, manpower and materials, and so assisted our war effort. The Board of Trade Make Do and Mend campaign is intended to help you get the last possible ounce of wear out of all your clothes and household things."

The booklet was filled with even more information and ideas for washing, regenerating, mending and making new clothes out of old. Making clothes last longer took up one chapter; washing and ironing hints took up another, while yet another was called "Turn Out and Renovate". Advice included:

"If you decide that the garment is quite unwearable, unpick it completely and with patience in order to salvage every inch of material; then wash it or send it to the cleaners. If the material is faded or patchy have it dyed a darker colour."

In the chapter "Unpick and Knit Again, New Life for Old Woollies" were included ideas on altering and revamping all sorts of knitwear, such as:

"Jumpers: Re-knit the sleeves in stripes, using up oddments of brightly-coloured wool, and make the new shaping at the top, thus giving it an extended shoulder-line. Add a striped pocket to match. A discarded jumper will make a child's jersey or frock. A 2-ply jumper in a pale colour would re-knit into a vest."

Making do and mending was nearly always a female job. Further ideas that emerged from the wealth of information and ideas that were printed included: how to prevent a skirt from "seating"; how to make slippers from an old felt hat; making taffeta rosettes or crocheting a frill to revive hats; fashioning new collars and cuffs on old blouses or dresses with fabric scraps, old lace or crocheted pieces; or even crocheting buttons for cardigans or painting the buttons on a coat, blouse or jacket in a different colour with nail polish. Maisie Walker recollects: "Fabric cut from the tail of a man's shirt could be used to recover a collar." Fiona Macdonald recalls: "My mother married in 1946 and – because of rationing (no coupons) – had to make slippers for her three bridesmaids out of scraps of left-over fabric stitched to cardboard insoles (early versions of the shoe insoles we can buy today). Mother said that parachute silk – often a very unseductive khaki – was tightly woven and extremely hot to wear. Like sitting a plastic bag, she said; it did not 'breathe'. She said that they also used to make new hats out of old hats or sometimes home-made artificial flowers plus scraps of net or tulle, held in place by hairpins." Everything was restricted to using the few materials that were available and various manufacturers and haberdashery suppliers capitalised on the problems through their advertising, such as:

"New Undies without Coupons the new 'dyeconomy' way. Practise economy the 'dyeconomy' way. It's the inexpensive simple way to bring new colourful life to dainty garments and fabrics. Auroral Cold Water Dyes eliminate boiling and give you new garments in two minutes."

Women did not just rely on the ideas they read about. Many also applied their own ingenuity in making new or smartening up old clothes. Bandages were cut and dyed to make hair bands and turbans (which were considered extremely chic); curtain fabric was used to make skirts, dresses or even coats; new jewellery was made from such things as beer bottle tops, buttons and corks; old blankets were turned into coats and jackets and old towels were made into children's dressing gowns. During the war parachute nylon (silk was difficult to obtain as it came from Asia) and parachute cord became available in certain areas for civilians as military surplus and later as a retail product. However it was acquired parachute silk and the harsher, newer nylon was used gleefully; cut down and made into underwear, nightwear, summer blouses or even wedding dresses. The Board of Trade issued a leaflet: "How to look after Parachute Nylon", which explained that the nylon appearing in the shops was parachute nylon and so not the better quality material they were expecting to have available within a relatively short time. Nylon was a new material, so the leaflet contained plenty of advice about washing, handling and sewing with it.

Utility clothing
Although clothes rationing began in June 1941, by the end of 1942, "Utility clothing" had also been introduced. With a strict set of guidelines laid down for their manufacture, the principle behind Utility clothing that it was standardised, so the government could ensure that all clothes were made with an absolute economy of raw materials and labour. Every garment was practical and simple, following certain regulations, such as narrow lapels, but especially:

- pleats, tucks, folds or gathers were restricted drastically
- no turn-ups on trousers
- no lace or embroidery trimmings
- similarly, no velvet, fur or leather trimmings
- ladies' skirts to be no longer than knee-length and straight
- no elastic waistbands or fancy belts on any ladies' clothes
- heels on ladies' shoes had to be less than two inches high
- no double-breasted men's jackets
- a maximum of three pockets were allowed on men's jackets
- a maximum of two pockets were allowed on men's trousers
- a maximum of three buttons were allowed on ladies' jackets

Even the fabrics had to conform to certain regulations. Cheaper wool mixtures, man-made rayon and cotton were all used for civilian clothes, leaving better quality cloth for uniforms. Clothing coupons were still required for Utility clothes; there was simply nothing else to buy unless it was second-hand. Successful and established designers such as Hardy Amies, Norman Hartnell, Berketex and Digby Morton were among those who designed ranges of Utility clothes, and so like Utility furniture, good design was not dispensed with. (Although some who wore the clothes would disagree with that.) Each designer produced designs for four simple outfits, including coats, suits and dresses and 32 of these were shown in London in September 1942, going on sale to the general public the following spring. All clothing carried the Utility mark: CC41, meaning Civilian Clothing 1941. In an attempt to rouse a sense of pride and patriotism despite these new restrictions, *Harper's Bazaar* noted that: "the backbone of morale is smartness; smartness and fashion are no longer synonymous." Similarly, in October 1942, *Vogue* wrote:

> "All women have a chance to buy beautifully designed clothes suitable to their lives and incomes. It [the Utility Scheme] is a revolutionary scheme and a heartening thought. It is, in fact, an outstanding example of applied democracy."

Although fabric was rationed and relatively basic (with the utility mark stamped on the edge), making clothes was cheaper than buying and the styles could be individually designed. But all clothes had to follow government patterns; even home-made clothing had to follow the Utility Scheme's strict rules of being plain and practical and not using up too much fabric, following the restrictions above.

Although not happy about the Utility Scheme or clothes rationing, in general, women did not complain as much as possibly expected. They tended to accept it as another challenge to their resourcefulness. The most surprising reaction was that many *men* complained profusely – and generally only over one main issue! In July 1943, the Board of Trade noted and commented publicly that men's tailors were frequently being pressed by their customers to evade Utility restrictions, specifically with regard to the ban on turn-ups. It became such an issue that angry debates were held in Parliament and letters of outrage were written to newspaper and magazine editors. Hugh Dalton refused to give way. Scathingly, in 1943, he declared: "There can be no equality of sacrifice in this war. Some must lose lives and limbs; others only the turn-ups on their trousers." In the same year, *The Times* printed a "Warning to Tailors". It began:

> "Offences against the Making of Civilian Clothing (Restrictions) Orders are so rife that the Board of Trade has decided that offenders will be summoned…"

The article went on to describe a tailor who had been prosecuted and who, in a statement to a Board of Trade inspector, had said: "I admit I have made about 45 to 50 suits in a non-austerity style during the past ten months, but if I had not done so my business would have ended. I only made these suits to oblige my customers." The tailor was not alone; it was found that many others were profiting by illicitly making trouser legs a few inches too long, so that purchasers could make their own turn-ups from the extra cloth.

Mrs Sew and Sew

Following on from the success of cartoon characters such as Potato Pete, the Board of Trade began using a little cartoon woman they called "Mrs Sew and Sew" to promote the Make Do and Mend campaign. Mrs Sew and Sew had a cotton reel body and clothes-peg legs. She explained such things as: "How to patch a shirt", "Keep them tidy underneath", "Smarten up your men" and "What Mother can do to save buying new". In conjunction with advertisements, leaflets, classes and demonstrations, short films were made by the Board of Trade and shown at the cinema before feature-length films.

In several leaflets, Mrs Sew and Sew reassuringly introduced topics that were often imperative, but that were not always understood. The little lady would appear on the front of the leaflets, so that readers were uplifted by her supportive face – knowing that if she was on the cover, the contents would be reliable and sensible. Inside the instructions were usually written in clear, step-by-step fashion. In one of her leaflets, called "Deft Darns", there were some "dos and don'ts" for "repairs that pay", such as:

- Do darn on the wrong side directly a thin place appears
- Do darn well beyond the weak place
- Don't wait for a hole to develop
- Don't make straight edges for your darns; a little irregularity distributes the strain

Save your shoes
One of the many leaflets produced by the Board of Trade featuring Mrs Sew and Sew was *Mrs Sew and Sew on Steps you can take to save your shoes*. This is an excerpt:

- Buy shoes wisely; remember that fit is more important than appearance
- New shoes will last longer if worn first on a dry day
- Give your shoes a rest; don't wear the same pair two days running if you can help it
- When you take off your shoes use shoe trees or stuff them with paper to keep the shape
- Damp shoes should be dried out slowly, never near strong heat
- Clean regularly; a little polish every time is better than a lot now and then
- See to repairs promptly, heels especially
- Rubber studs, rubber soles and iron tips will help shoes to wear longer

---

Sharing, swapping and second-hand
Selling rationed items for money was categorised as black market, for which there could be a prison sentence, but swapping, sharing or buying second-hand goods were all legal. Most newsagents and Post Offices had postcards displayed in their windows saying things like:

Boy's shoes, black, size 5, hardly worn, swap for large tablecloth
Baby's cot, swap for men's trousers
Floral tea set, four cups and saucers, swap for woman's raincoat

Many shopkeepers began a sideline in selling second-hand clothes – and several enterprising and practical women made businesses out of their creative abilities. Jean Turner's mum made a living "turning coats". Jean explained:

"My mum was very clever at making do and mending and she became well known for this in our neighbourhood. With all her alterations and clever mending, she was running a business from our front room. People brought her their old coats, which she paid for, then she turned the coats inside out and using the inside (the parts that had been protected by lining) as the outside, she cut out and made new coats for children, which she then sold."

Voluntary organisations such as the Women's Institute and the WVS gave classes and demonstrations in towns and villages across the country. These gatherings were focal points for many and served as excellent forums for sharing ideas. Pat Fox remembers:

"I used to go to the Women's Institute meeting once a fortnight with my mother in a church hall. One of the ladies usually gave a demonstration on making or repairing something. I particularly remember how to knit a soft toy or – this must sound a bit strange – how to knit pretend 'icing' for a cake! Afterwards, the women used to discuss what they could do with threadbare coats, worn shoes or fraying cardigans."

The Board of Trade leaflet, *A Guide to Woollies*, included a lot of extremely useful tips, including a section on "Special Tips for Home Knitters". Some of the advice in that section included:

"A one plain, one purl single rib is better for boys' wear than stocking stitch.
If possible, use new wool for the welt, when you are re-knitting old wool for the body of the garment. Old wool hasn't enough elasticity for a firm welt.
When casting on, put the needle behind instead of through

stitches. This makes a firm edge, so there is no need to knit into back of stitches in first row."

Most towns had WVS shoe and clothing exchanges too. These were set up by members of the WVS wherever they could, in outhouses, Town Halls, community centres, empty shops or offices – anywhere they could put a rack of clothes and people could come in and try on the clothes. It proved to be an invaluable service, especially for mothers with children who were outgrowing their clothes before the garments were worn out. WVS clothing exchanges worked on a points system; mothers brought in clothes they could not use and items were awarded a certain number of points, which could be used to "purchase" more suitable items of clothing. Many women got together anyway, meeting in each other's homes and swapping clothes and other household items, or renovating things that were becoming worn or outgrown.

Wedding dresses were one item of clothing that became scarce early on. Old wedding dresses were usually swapped, (often at the WVS clothing exchanges), and worn several times, borrowed by sisters and friends. At first, white weddings were considered by many to be inappropriate extravagances and even rather distasteful in the circumstances. Then later in the war, more brides aimed to make their weddings as close to peacetime occasions as possible to boost morale and make things feel more "normal". (In 1938, 409,000 people were married in Britain. By 1940 the number had risen to 495,000, as couples made their relationships more permanent in such an uncertain world.) Yet of course, organising weddings was incredibly difficult, so unless they were in uniform, wartime brides usually wore a simple suit or dress and a plain hat. Many added a small corsage of white flowers pinned to the lapel.

Stockings, shoes and siren suits

From 1940 the production of silk and nylon stockings stopped in Britain as they were both needed for parachutes. Unless they were brought into the country by returning or visiting members of the armed forces, silk stockings were simply no longer available. It is quite legendary that this small luxury was generally the one that women missed the most. The densely knitted lisle stockings that were intended to replace them were universally disliked and many women wore ankle socks instead. Stockings were one item that if they became available on the black market, were highly sought after and are one of the reasons that the American soldiers were so popular with British women. (But only one; with their flattering uniforms, glamorous Hollywood-sounding accents, and supplies of other goods, including branded cosmetics, gum, sweets and money, they seemed like romantic heroes to many local girls.) Young British women who befriended American soldiers often received nylon stockings as gifts from them, which being unavailable in British shops were considered precious commodities. Pretty underwear was not available either, and the only way that feminine lingerie or nightwear could be obtained was for women to make it for themselves. If parachute silk or nylon could not be found, enterprising females used anything from pillowcases or sheets to muslin, eiderdowns, old wedding dresses or pre-war corsets. One of the biggest problems was the lack of elastic; along with silk and nylon, it was extremely difficult to find. Additionally, fewer colours were used for dyeing wartime clothing, as many of the chemicals needed for dyeing were also used in explosives and other indispensable resources needed for the war.

The government tried to promote the idea of wearing clogs as hardwearing, sturdy shoes with wooden soles that did not require much leather, but these were never popular. Unexpectedly, wedge shoes with cork soles caught on. Cork was light, slightly springy, available, long-lasting, fairly cheap and comfortable to wear. Because the wedge softened the effects of walking on hard surfaces, they allowed women to walk for miles. A tip for making shoes last longer was to paint the soles with varnish. Another rather unexpected fashion that emerged was the siren suit. These were all-in-one jumpsuits, similar to boiler suits and they became popular attire for all to wear during air raids. Perfect for speed dressing and for keeping warm, they could be put on over children's pyjamas and rapidly zipped up at the sound of a siren. Adults and children wore them; even the Princesses Elizabeth and Margaret and Winston Churchill. Yvonne Gilan remembers:

"My grandmother made my siren suit. Siren suits were given their name because when a siren sounded, mothers could quickly put their children into them over whatever we were wearing that day. Just a quick zip up and off we went."

Over the siren suit some people wore a Kangaroo cloak. Not as popular as the siren suit, this was a warm cloak made of one or two pieces of material – often old blankets – with huge, roomy pockets, which were extremely practical for keeping all sorts of things in to be taken into air raid shelters.

The *Make Do and Mend leaflet No. 4*, "What Mothers can do to Save Buying New" showed how to reinforce children's clothes; how to let out and lengthen children's clothes, hints on cutting new clothes for children and cutting down grown-ups' clothes for children. In "How to Let Out and Lengthen Children's Clothes", ideas included: "As a general rule…the outgrown article should be completely unpicked from hem to underarm each side, and then along the sleeve seam, until the whole garment can be opened out flat in one piece."

In 1943, Hugh Dalton – who was never as popular as Lord Woolton – wrote to the public in a press advertisement. Entitled "To All of You", the letter began:

"Two years of clothes rationing have come and gone. There are 600,000 fewer workers making civilian clothes than before the war. That is a saving of man-power of which we can all be proud. To all of you who have so cheerfully made-do, who have mended and managed and got months of extra wear out of your own, your husband's and your children's clothes, I say thank you."

He wrote further messages in more leaflets that same year, including:

"Remember that every coupon unspent means less strain on the country's resources. To wear clothes that have been patched and darned – perhaps many times – is to show oneself a true patriot….Making-do may at times seem a little dreary. Nearly every woman, and some men, would like something new to wear. But, even when old clothes aren't exciting, they are a war-winning fashion, to follow which will speed the day of victory."

In yet another leaflet, also from 1943, Hugh Dalton wrote: "We want to help you get the last possible ounce of wear out of your clothes and household things." The hints and tips included were practical and useful, and are still valuable for today. Such as:

Tips on taking care of clothes
1. Mend clothes before washing them as a tear or hole may become unmanageable. Keep a look out for loose buttons and other fastenings, frayed buttonholes and split seams, and mend them at once. Save all tapes, ribbons, buttons, hooks and eyes and keep a well-stocked work basket.
2. Cover all shoulders of clothes on hangers with a collar of newspaper to make them last longer. Shut wardrobe doors firmly to keep moths out.
3. Repair shoes as soon as they need it and never walk down the heels. Never dry shoes near heat as it will ruin the leather.
4. Change into old clothes when you're at home, and give the clothes you have just taken off an airing before putting them away.
5. Don't throw your things down in a heap when you take them off. While they are still warm, the material will crease. Brush them with a short-haired brush…and shake them well. Then hang them on hangers, making sure that the hangers are wide enough…Do up all fastenings before hanging clothes. This helps them to keep their shape.
6. Remove all stains at once as they usually come out fairly easily before they are set. For grease, use a hot iron on a piece of clean white blotting paper placed over the stain. For all other stains, try plain tepid water first, and then soap and water.
7. Don't wear clothes and shoes day after day, as a rest does them good.
8. Never let clothes get really dirty. Dirt injures fabric, so clean or wash clothes when slightly soiled.

Tips to save you time and trouble

In one of the leaflets called "Turn out and Renovate", further useful tips were suggested in a section called "Tips to save you time and trouble". These included:

If you particularly like any part of a garment such as the sleeves or neckline, make a paper pattern of it for future use;

Unless you are an expert, never attempt to cut out without using a paper pattern;

When you choose a pattern, be sure the size conforms to your up-to-date measurements;

Be very careful about mixing materials…don't mix together materials that require different washing treatment.

Bundles for Britain

The British War Relief Society (BWRS) was a US-based charitable organisation that arranged the supply of non-military aid such as food, clothes, medical supplies and financial aid to people in Britain during the conflict. One charity that did not come under the administration of the BWRS however, was "Bundles for Britain". It began in December 1941, when a Californian philanthropist, Marion Jorgensen, asked her friends to knit garments for British sailors who sailed back and forth across the Atlantic on war missions. The knitting was such a success that Jorgensen began to send further medical supplies and other necessary items to refugees and victims of bombing when the Blitz started. The "Bundles for Britain" scheme as it became known was exceptionally helpful in raising morale in Britain. A Pathé news bulletin of March 1941, showing various close-ups of people trying on clothes ran:

"Big consignments of clothes for victims of the Blitz are now arriving in Britain from the USA. At a distribution centre in Docklands, men and women who have suffered at the hands of Hitler's killers try on articles of clothing that will help to replace the things they have lost. American parents whose children sleep safely, have contributed largely to relieve things over here with money and clothing…helpers at the settlement can usually find something for everybody. Hundreds of war-impoverished people are grateful to kind-hearted Americans for their help."

Many victims of the Blitz suffered from depression, having often lost everything they owned from German bombs. The thought that American well-wishers had thought of them and sent them some practical and useful gifts was often immensely helpful in lifting that depression. Joan Easton remembered:

"To know that compassionate and sympathetic people had cared enough to send us clothes and other things we might need – and to actually be given some new clothes helped cheer up so many families. At the centre, I remember the atmosphere was very bright and fun. The gifts of clothes and other necessary items gave us and very many other families the courage to face our troubles once more."

7
DOING THEIR BIT

"Your Courage, Your Cheerfulness, Your Resolution, Will Bring Us Victory." ~ Ministry of Information poster, 1939

At the outbreak of war in 1939, the government formed the Ministry of Information as a department to be responsible for publicity and propaganda, to boost the morale of the public and to make sure that the "right" information was distributed. Located in Senate House at the University of London, at its height, 3,000 people worked in the department, producing posters, films, radio broadcasts, pamphlets, newspaper articles and press advertisements, but at first, it was not successful. Much of the publicity and propaganda came across as patronising and pompous as the writers recruited did not always appreciate the feelings of the people, and they were often heavy-handed and long-winded. Additionally, leaflets dropped into Germany were full of grammatical and spelling errors. But as the war went on, the Ministry learned what would appeal to the public. A huge opinion survey called Mass Observation regularly recorded people's opinions and feelings, revealing what would win them over more effectively. One surprising and unexpected technique that was learned quite early on was to relate bad news as well as good. It was discovered that when they heard bad news, people were more inclined to accept the plausibility of everything, and being aware of the lows as well as the highs also helped them to cope with disappointments. Nevertheless, certain news items were withheld because the government thought they would crush public spirit. For example, reports of ships sunk by Japanese kamikaze pilots were not reported; certain photos were prohibited from being publicised, such as any of dead children and one of a bomb that had crashed into a London Underground station; in 1941, the Communist newspaper *The Daily Worker* was banned as it opposed the war; soldiers' letters were censored with all mention of times and places deleted and the invention of radar was not mentioned, instead the notion that eating carrots helped RAF pilots see in the dark, was made known.

Keep Calm and Carry On

In April 1939, ahead of time, in an effort to raise morale and to motivate everyone when war broke out, the Ministry of Information commissioned three posters. In flat, bold and bright colours, they featured the shape of George VI's crown (to reassure the public that the King was with them) and, in a clear sans serif font, bore the slogans: "Your Courage, Your Cheerfulness, Your Resolution Will Bring Us Victory", "Freedom is in Peril, Defend It with All Your Might", and "Keep Calm and Carry On". The first two posters were displayed as prominently as possible: on public transport, in shop windows and on notice boards and hoardings across Britain. But the "Keep Calm and Carry On" poster was never released. It remained virtually unknown until a bookshop owner discovered one in a box of old books he bought at auction in 2000. The Ministry of Information's plan had been to issue the poster only in times of crisis, specifically the invasion of Britain by Germany. As this did not happen, the posters were never officially used and at the end of the war they were all collected up and pulped. Meanwhile, the poster "Your Courage, Your Cheerfulness, Your Resolution Will Bring Us Victory" annoyed people! Because of the wording, it was perceived that there was a "them" and an "us". It seemed that "us" was the government and it was expecting everyone to make sacrifices and work for it, not for the good of all. The two posters were not used for long.

Another unsuccessful campaign included a poster with the headline: "Don't do it Mother – Leave the Children Where they Are". The poster featured a mother sitting next to a tree, her two little boys playing in front of her, while behind them all, in sinister, ghostly outline, Hitler bent over, whispering, "Take them back!" The poster was intended to make mothers leave their evacuated children in the country rather than take them back to the towns again, but it had the opposite effect; making mothers miss their children even more and want to protect them. To put the point across, the poster was reinforced by magazines. For instance, in 1941, the editor of *Woman's Own* published an article that began: "If your children have an opportunity of going off to the country, don't grudge it to them because you will be lonely…Apart from their health – and none of you can deny that space and fresh air and country food are best for growing boys and girls – they will benefit enormously from new experiences and friendships."

The BBC played its part in the propaganda and publicity machine throughout the war too. In 1939 it was expanded hugely, with several new broadcasts following, most of which helped to raise morale. Before the war, BBC newsreaders simply announced "This is the news from London" but during the war, they developed the habit of starting the news by saying: "Here is the news; and this is [newsreader's name – such as Alvar Lidell or Bruce Belfrage] reading it." This was so that listeners would learn to recognise genuine BBC newsreaders' voices and so would be able to tell immediately if an enemy should feign to be a newsreader. Strict standards demanded that any BBC announcers were always dressed smartly – even when they would not be seen by their audiences. This even stretched to wearing full evening dress if the type of programme demanded it.

Black propaganda

Black propaganda emerged on both sides during the war. It was a method of trying to confuse and demoralise the enemy by sending false messages to its civilians. Intended to disrupt the foe's resolve to fight, both Britain and Germany indulged in it. On the first day of the war, the British dropped leaflets over Germany and during the course of the war, millions of publications were created by the Ministry of Information and released over Nazi-occupied Europe, including leaflets, newspapers, stickers, stamps and posters – in various languages, such as French, German, Danish, Norwegian, and Czech.

One of the most well-known examples of black propaganda in Britain was "Lord Haw-Haw". This was the Irish-American William Joyce, who lived in Britain before the war, carried a British passport and had joined the British Union of Fascists under Oswald Mosley. When war broke out, in fear of being detained by the British authorities, he and his wife Margaret fled to Germany in August 1939. He became a naturalised German in 1940 and from September 1939 worked for German radio, broadcasting black propaganda every night to Britain aiming to frighten and dishearten the British people. His broadcasts "informed" the British that the war was hopeless and that they were being defeated, but his nasal voice and exaggerated upper-class accent became recognised and his opening line "This is 'Jairmany' calling" inspired a journalist on *The Daily Express* to call him Lord Haw-Haw. The nickname stuck. Those who remember describe his "sneering, smarmy, creepy voice" that was "posh, like a lecturer", "insidious" and "full of vindictive pleasure about what was going to happen to the British". There were actually at least three men who broadcast from that news channel and were nicknamed Lord Haw-Haw collectively, but Joyce was the most notorious. There were several other broadcasts from Berlin that could be picked up in Britain, with a wide range of programmes that highlighted the positives about Germany, but the news channel was the most listened to. Its popularity arose partly because at the beginning of the war, the BBC was extremely dreary, with no humour or popular music. It did not have mass appeal and many described it as being tedious and soporific. Some remembered tuning into German radio stations: "It was thrilling really to have contact with the enemy. We lived such simple, narrow lives." Although listening to the nightly broadcast was discouraged by the British authorities, it was estimated that early on in the war, approximately six million people tuned in to hear Lord Haw-Haw every night; mainly to laugh at his accent and spiteful claims, although some declared that there was "a great deal of truth" in what he said. His broadcasts were overtly anti-Semitic, they ridiculed Winston Churchill and they made many feel unsettled and uncertain, so in July 1940, the British government issued a warning as part of an information campaign which appeared in the press and always began with: "What do I do if?" This one read:

"What do I do if... I come across German or Italian broadcasts when tuning in my wireless? I say to myself: 'Now this blighter wants me to listen to him. Am I going to do what he wants? ...I remember nobody can trust a word the Haw-Haws say, so just to make them waste their time, I switch 'em off or tune 'em out!'"

From the middle of 1940, when things became particularly bleak in Britain and the possibility of defeat was faced, the popularity of Lord Haw-Haw's broadcasts diminished. After the war, Joyce was arrested by British Military Police and taken to London where he was tried and found guilty of treason. He was hanged in 1946.

With the main part of the Ministry of Information's role being to reassure the public and keep up morale throughout the war selected MoI workers were sent to listen to conversations in pubs, cafés and shops and on trains and buses. These were reported back to headquarters and from them, more targeted publicity was prepared. In 1940 it became an offence, punishable by a £50 fine, to pass on any rumour "likely to cause alarm and despondency". The government impressed upon all that it was everyone's duty to discourage unfounded gossip whether in public or in private. In contrast, a positive attitude was encouraged as an important aspect of the war effort, as Churchill, among many others, believed that this would create an indomitable resistance against the enemy. To this end, the government declared that listening to enemy radio propaganda should be ridiculed and vehemently discouraged. In speeches and in press advertisements, ministers urged everyone to be mindful of what they listened to or said. The Ministry of Information launched an anti-rumour campaign with a newspaper announcement:

"Warning: Do not discuss anything which might be of national importance. The consequence of any such indiscretion may be the loss of many lives."

This was closely followed by the "Careless Talk Costs Lives" campaign, which consisted of several humorous posters, many drawn by the *Punch* cartoonist Cyril Kenneth Bird (1887-1965), who worked under the name Fougasse. Best known for being the art editor at *Punch* from 1937 to 1949, Fougasse also worked for the Ministry of Information throughout the war for free, (for which he was awarded a CBE in 1946). His amusing posters were extremely popular; the simple line drawings were witty, succinct and almost irreverent, which made everyone smile.

Another cartoon that made a regular appearance in newspapers from 1941 and cheered everyone up was Mr Chad. John Hubbard remembered: "Mr Chad was a cartoon face with a long nose, peering over a fence who always moaned. Everything he said began with 'WOT, no...?' Because he was such a grumpy old thing, he made everyone laugh about the shortages. It was as if he was moaning for all of us. There he would be, in the papers, looking long-faced and saying things like: 'WOT, no oranges?' 'WOT, no sugar?' 'WOT, no bread?' It made it feel all right to be secretly fed up about things, even though you'd never let on – or risk seeming unpatriotic. After all, if the soldiers, sailors and airmen could risk their lives every day, a few shortages could be put up with at home."

Catchphrases
But it was not just cartoons that made people smile and kept them focused on "doing their bit" for the war effort. Tommy Handley, a comedian, became a regular broadcaster with the BBC, inspiring listeners to use the catchphrases from his most popular show, *ITMA* (which came from its original title, *It's That Man Again*). The show made fun of practically every aspect of British wartime life, including the Ministry of Works. Every character was a parody of the types of people who were encountered daily, such as the constantly inebriated Colonel Chinstrap who replied to anything he thought was an alcoholic drink with: "I don't mind if I do", or the cleaning lady, Mrs Mopp with her, "Can I do you now, Sir?" More of the catchphrases that came from the show included: "TTFN" (ta-ta for now); "It's being so cheerful as keeps me going", and "Don't forget the diver". Catchphrases were unheard of before the war, but Tommy Handley's characters became defined by them and the idea that saying a few words that were really quite meaningless, but that could raise a smile anywhere in the country, helped to brighten everyone. It was further

common ground, a way of connecting with others, even complete strangers, which made it comforting. The popular advertising slogans added to this and there were many others, including: "Put that light out", "Don't you know there's a war on" and "Doing your bit". Catchphrases caught on and formed part of everyday conversation, stirring the hearts of all those on the Home Front, reinforcing their courage and their determination to keep going.

Crime

Although most people used their own creativity and enterprise to keep going and support each other, some used it simply to help themselves. From 1939 to 1945, the crime rate in Britain increased by 57 per cent. With a reduced police force, blackouts and rationing, there was plenty of opportunity for law-breaking. Bombed homes were looted by the unscrupulous. Some rushed straight into bombed properties – whether private homes or shops – and helped themselves, while others were more opportunist and picked things up that had been scattered in the streets by bombs. The particularly calculating dressed up as ARP wardens and stole items from the homes and people they were meant to be rescuing, or took valuables from the dead or dying. With everyone else so busy trying to pull together and help each other, relatively few of these criminals were caught and punished. Enemies without were the focus, not enemies within. In November 1940 *The Daily Mirror* published an article: "Hang a Looter and Stop This Filthy Crime!" but little could be done with resources so stretched anyway. There were strong feelings of horror that people could act in this way, but little that anyone could do to stop it. Because rationing made everyone so desperate, some thieves calculated stealing goods that were particularly sought after, while others were more opportunistic. Some doctors took bribes to sign people off as unfit to serve in the armed forces and some disabled people accepted money to attend medicals of those who had their received call-up papers, effectively excusing healthy people from active service. During the Blitz the government paid £500 to those who had lost their homes through bombing, plus additional compensation for damaged or lost furniture and clothing. Many unscrupulous individuals claimed the compensation by pretending that they had suffered in this way. The authorities often suspected, but had no time to investigate. The blackout enabled both pickpockets and prostitutes to flourish. Prostitutes particularly profited from the thousands of soldiers departing for the Front. Maggie Stewart, who worked in the Ministry of Labour in London recalled:

"During the war, everyone had to register for war work or the services, but it was difficult to categorise prostitutes. The services wouldn't take them and if you sent them to a factory, none of the girls would mix with them or use the same facilities. Mothers of girls from upper-class and aristocratic families wrote complaining letters that their daughters were being forced to associate with prostitutes. So they could not be placed. It didn't take long for the lazier individuals to cotton on that prostitution was a way out of working. It became quite a desirable business to be in!"

The crime rate rose because of the desperate needs of everybody and even those who believed themselves to be honest were often guilty of buying goods or spare ration coupons on the black market. The sellers of black market goods became known as "spivs" or "wide-boys". Often selling their items out of suitcases, which could be snapped shut in seconds if a policeman came along, they made huge profits. Most were of little consequence in comparison to contemporary events, but some was quite far-reaching. In 1943, in one operation, five million clothing coupons were stolen and the government had to cancel the entire issue. Crime was not completely ignored however and by the end of the war more than 114,000 prosecutions for black market activities had taken place, sometimes for surprisingly minor offences. No one was exempt from punishment. In fact, many were used as examples. In 1944 the composer Ivor Novello was sentenced to eight weeks' imprisonment – which was subsequently reduced to four – for using extra petrol coupons given to him by a female fan. Yet even though criminal activities increased, the streets of Britain did not descend into lawlessness and the majority of British people got through the war honestly and with a united front.

Children

Often separated from their parents through evacuation, the armed forces or bereavement, in general, children were remarkably resilient and exceptionally helpful. They saved, collected, made and sold, all to help the war effort and generally faced the difficulties as resolutely as their parents.

In the prelude to the war, the government prepared the evacuation programme by dividing the country into three types of area: Evacuation, Neutral and Reception. Evacuation areas were particularly important locations or industrial areas that would be likely targets for enemy bombers, while reception areas were rural places that were considered relatively safe, such as Kent, Wales, Derbyshire and East Anglia. Of the five and a half million who met the criteria for the evacuation scheme, only about 30 per cent actually went, but even so, it caused huge disruptions to both the families who were separated and those who took in evacuees. Anne Maltby remembers the day she was evacuated with her school to New Mills in Derbyshire on 1st September 1939.

"My elder sister Jean and I went to the same school, so I don't remember being sad about leaving our mum. But I do remember being thrilled about the train ride and eating a tomato sandwich on the journey! Looking back, our mother must have been distraught, but we accepted it all, we weren't aware of the dangers then. When we arrived in New Mills, we were all herded into the playground of a school where local ladies came up to us and literally picked who they liked the look of. I was the same size as one woman's daughter, so I suppose she thought it would be a good idea to take me in. She said, 'I'll have that one,' as if she was choosing sweets. I panicked and clung to my sister and luckily one of our teachers (they were all evacuated with us) told the woman, 'I'm sorry, she has to go with her sister.' Another lady took us both, but I hated every minute of the evacuation and was very happy to return home a few months later."

On the other side of things, Peter Jones was an only child living in Tredegar, Wales. In 1939 he was 13 when his mother took in an evacuee from London and he hated having to share for the first time! Fortunately the boy did not stay long and in the next phase of evacuation the following summer, Peter and his friends were ready to throw stones at a train that was rumoured to be bringing a school of boys to Tredegar. Peter's daughter recounted the story: "The Tredegar boys all lined up, ready to attack the evacuated boys, but when the train arrived and the doors opened…it was a girls' school! Suddenly, the evacuees were very welcome!"

Those in London had to deal with all eventualities. In about 1941 when Stan Bell was walking to school in Hackney, a German pilot flew quite low and began shooting:

> "I was walking across Clapton Common. There were lots of other people about, going to school and work. The German plane flew down – he must have been a rogue pilot as he began shooting at us with a machine gun. Everyone ran and sheltered where we could until he had passed. Fortunately, he was too high to hit anyone."

Early on in the war, Jean Pink had been terrified of both gas masks and barrage balloons, but she said:

> "The doodlebugs, which came later in the war, were the most frightening of all the bombs. They flew independently, with no pilots and then dropped on civilians. They first attacked London in June 1944. You could hear their loud buzzing sound as they came towards you, which stopped suddenly when they were about to drop. It was terrifying when you heard the buzz and even worse when it stopped. Other bombs that the Germans dropped later in the war were known as butterfly bombs because they were quite small and had wings. A butterfly bomb didn't explode on impact but only if someone touched it as it lay on the ground. They looked like toys, so policemen came to my school to warn us about the dangers and tell us not to touch them. Articles were printed in newspapers to warn us about them too."

Although London was the most bombed of all British cities, Hull was the second most severely targeted, with 95 per cent of houses damaged or destroyed over the course of the war. One evening early in 1941, John Maltby, a child living in Lincolnshire, was walking along a country path. "Where I lived was high enough to see across to the River Humber, but one night I was out and could see as far as Hull, it was so brightly illuminated by all the incendiary bombs. It was shocking to witness, but we were desensitised to the horrors of war as they came daily."

Many children were more upset by their pets' distress than by anything else. Gas masks were produced for horses, but they were expensive, and none were produced for any other animal, although the RSPCA produced a leaflet advising on ways of keeping pets calm, including padding dogs' ears with cotton wool and tying a mask across their eyes. The leaflet stated that "few cats would tolerate anything of the kind". Anne Maltby recollected: "My father was in the First World War so had experience of digging trenches. He and my two brothers dug a trench in our back garden, lined the floor with planks of wood and put a vertical ladder on the side. They made a 'lid' for it too. As soon as the air raid siren sounded, my dog would run down! Don't ask me how he managed the vertical ladder, but he did – both ways, down and then up after the air raid!"

Yvonne Gilan who was eight years old when the war broke out, raised money for wartime causes:

"My mother made me a tray with pink ribbon round my neck and I went to all the neighbours' houses, selling lavender bags, bath salts in pink net bags, felt pen-wipers – because we used fountain pens then and the ink often needed wiping – spills (for lighting gas fires) in painted boxes, string shopping bags, pin cushions, handkerchiefs embroidered with little crinoline ladies (very popular) and decorated candles. Sometimes my friend Kathleen came with me. I sent the money I made to Clementine Churchill for her War Fund and she sent me a letter thanking me for it....which I still have. Everything on the tray was made by my grandmother, my mother, my Aunt Netta and especially my beloved godmother, Aunt Mary."

Yvonne explained how her mother, grandmother and aunts were exceptionally creative:

"They were hoarders, you see, so anything they had was used, any bits of wool, ribbons, net. They knitted, sewed and used up everything. I used to make cotton reel mats. It's called French knitting nowadays and I did it with wooden cotton reels. It was such fun when the knitting started to come through the bottom of the reel. Once I'd made a long enough piece, I finished it off and coiled it into spirals to make the mats."

Yvonne's Coil Mats
A wooden cotton reel
Four nails
Wool
Needle and thread
Crochet hook

1. *Press the four nails into the top of the cotton reel.*
2. *Thread the wool through the cotton reel from top to bottom.*
3. *Wind the wool twice around the nails in an anti-clockwise direction. Do not pull it too tightly.*
4. *With the crochet hook, lift one strand of wool up and over the other strand and each nail. Continue working in this way, going round and round, hooking wool over each nail and previous stitch an anti-clockwise direction and as it emerges from the bottom, tug the knitted cord gently.*
5. *If you want to change wool colour, simply cut and tie a new coloured wool to the previous colour, but make sure that the knot is pushed inside the nails.*
6. *When your cord is long enough, cut the wool, leaving a short length and thread it through each loop. Pull tight to fasten off.*
7. *To make a coil mat, curl the knitted cord in a flat spiral and stitch it together.*

Jackie Watson remembers going regularly with a friend to neighbours' houses, pushing a wheelbarrow and collecting people's paper and glass salvage, and then wheeling the full barrow on to a WVS collection centre. In 1941 the Ministry of Information issued a leaflet especially for 14 to 18 year olds. Headed: "You can help your country", it explained:

"The difference between this war and the previous wars is that now we are all in the Front Line in a struggle for the principles of freedom and justice and respect for the laws of God and honour amongst men. Whether we are in uniform or not, we are in the war. And no matter how young we are or how old we are, there are jobs we can do for our country."

The leaflet suggested ways these young people could help, such as taking charge of some of the air raid precautions in their home; learning how to deal with a gas leak or a burnt-out electric fuse; cooking some meals; becoming the main salvage collector in the home; growing vegetables; helping elderly or invalid neighbours; learning first aid and making splints and bandages. They were urged to work hard; to be careful what they said; keep smiling; keep fit; save all they could and to be as independent as they could. By the end of 1941 it became compulsory for everyone aged 16 to 18 to join a youth group. Committees were established to advise on the most suitable groups for each individual. National youth groups with local branches included: The Red Cross Society and the St John's Ambulance Brigade, Scouts and Cubs, Girl Guides and Rangers, Boys' Brigade, the Air Training Corps and Women's Junior Air Corps, but there were also many others. In general, youth groups were places where young people met and socialised, but they also learned useful skills, such as first aid, nursing and handicrafts (girls only), how to help with the Civil Defence, some learned unarmed combat and had weapons training (boys only).

Schools participated wholeheartedly in the war effort, some adopting particular military units for example, as they raised money, saved, collected, grew vegetables and donated. Some schools started "Spitfire" or "Warship Funds". By raising money for these named causes, schoolchildren could learn how much of the money they had saved would buy something essential for the war like a Spitfire or warship. It was important that along with the adults, children felt as if they were making a difference. In 1940, more than 6,000 school savings groups started. Rosemary Winters recalled:

"We were encouraged to save regularly at school by buying Savings Stamps, which were stuck into our savings books. During the war everyone was encouraged not to spend money frivolously but to put as much as possible into National Savings by way of stamps which were 6d each, or Savings Certificates which cost 15 shillings with interest after five years to help pay for the war. Thirty savings stamps could be exchanged for a Certificate. Every school, organisation and business set their own target for special weeks such as 'Spitfire Week', 'Support our Soldiers' and 'Warship Week'. At our school, we 'adopted' a ship and wrote letters to the sailors on board."

Boys were taught to be useful in the woodwork department while girls were taught to knit or sew and make things to send to the Front and to help their families. Toys were in short supply as materials were scarce, being needed for more essential wartime items. Many toys were either home-made or second-hand, as a new business emerged, known as "toy exchanges" where children (or parents) either swapped or sold toys they no longer wanted. Most home-made toys were knitted or sewn, or made of paper, card, tin or off-cuts of wood. Jean Pink remembered how early on in the war she read Enid Blyton's *Sunny Stories* and later *Girl's Crystal*. She played with her rag doll and was happy to cut out paper dolls and their separate clothes, attaching the clothes to the dolls by folding tabs or doing cotton reel knitting. She also remembered making pompoms using wool and milk bottle tops. During the war, milk bottles were wider at the neck and the tops were made of circular card with a small central push-out hole. Jean explained:

"We'd put two milk bottle tops together and wound wool around them through the central hole, round and round over and again until the hole was closed up and the card circles could no longer be seen. Then we cut round the outer edge of wool and tied another piece of wool between the two pieces of card so the bulk of the wool was held tightly in the centre. We took away the two circles of card and fluffed out the pompom!"

The BBC catered for children with its daily (half-hour) programme, *Children's Hour*, which ran competitions to encourage children to help with the war effort and there were also two schools' programmes each day during the week. Comics were still produced, the favourites including *Sunny Stories*, *Girl's Crystal*, *The Beano* and *The Dandy*, although like newspapers and magazines, they were subject to paper shortages and diminished in size. Children's books were still produced and enjoyed by many, including Richmal Crompton's *Just William*, who became involved in numerous wartime scrapes, while Enid Blyton continued to produce various books for children of all ages, including *Five O'Clock Tales*, *The Famous Five* and the boarding school stories of *St Clare's*, which ignored the war completely. But childhood did not last long. Most children left school at 14 and went straight to work. By 18 the majority were conscripted for the services or for war work. Joan Easton remembered: "*Everyone* was asked to help win the war by making extra efforts and working harder and on the whole, everyone did."

Cardboard cakes

As restrictions and shortages increased, everyone had to work harder and be more innovative. Along with many other sayings and catchphrases, the mottoes "be thankful and never grumble" and "never leave any food on your plate" were often uttered. With so many severe restraints and deficiencies, these positive aphorisms helped to keep people focused. At some moments, things became so bad that everyone's resilience and fortitude was tested and sometimes in unexpectedly trivial areas. In July 1940, coming soon after the Battle of Dunkirk, the making or selling of iced cakes was banned. It was just a small thing in the umpteen other hardships and sorrows, but iced cakes were such a symbolic part of some of the happiest of occasions in British life, such as weddings and christenings, that it disheartened many. As usual, creativity came to the fore. Within a short time, smaller plain cakes were made for weddings and other such celebrations, covered with simulated icing – often cardboard tiers (like upside-down hat boxes) that resembled real icing, while some made knitted 'icing' covers, that looked rather like tea cosies. If there was to be a reception, usually friends and relatives helped by saving and pooling food coupons, but even so, refreshments were always frugal.

Few newlyweds took honeymoons, and family holidays were rare. The beaches of the South and East coast were barricaded with barbed wire and their hotels were mainly requisitioned for military use, so these pre-war destinations became almost out of bounds. In 1942 the government introduced the "Holidays at Home" scheme, encouraging people to find things they could do locally rather than travelling far away. Employees did not have time off for holidays as in peacetime and anyway, there were travel restrictions. Special cheap day and weekend excursions were organised by bus and railway companies, although these were mainly to help parents who were trying to visit their evacuated children. The Holidays at Home scheme was run by local councils who put on concerts, parties, fairs and other forms of local entertainment. Thousands also responded to a government campaign to take working holidays on farms. Margaret Ronaldson who lived in Bow, London, recalled: "Even if holidays hadn't been cancelled during the war, we'd never have been able to afford to go away, so we were pleased to go and work on a farm. We went to the same one in Kent every year for about four days each time. There must have been over a hundred people staying there, all doing the same. Some stayed for two weeks. It was hard work, but lots of fresh air, everyone was cheery and the food was marvellous and every night, we all had a sing-song! It was a wonderful atmosphere."

With so many people away – in the services, evacuated, in the Land Army or nursing – letter writing was an important aspect of the war. To help everyone in what could sometimes become a difficult task, advice on letter writing was printed in newspapers and magazines. In September 1940, *Good Housekeeping* printed an article written by the highly-respected writer Daphne du Maurier, whose best-selling novel *Rebecca* had been published in 1938. This is a small excerpt from her article entitled "Letter Writing in Wartime":

"…Any murmur of 'self-pity' will not be helpful to the writer. The woman who dares to write: 'This agony of separation is too much for me to bear' cannot be forgiven. Whatever she does, and must feel in her heart, of strain and anxiety, no sign of it should appear in any of her letters. Men are not always the sturdy, stalwart creatures we imagine and a yearning letter from home may bring the nervy, highly-strung type to breaking-point."

It was not just the "nervy, highly-strung type" who was considered, but the entire British nation. It was imperative that everyone kept positive and confident. This was all an essential part of "doing your bit". Apart from a short time in the summer of 1940, everyone in Britain firmly believed that they would win the war.

8
HOME LIFE

"This is not the end. It is not even the beginning of the end. But it is, perhaps, the end of the beginning." ~ Winston Churchill, November 1942

Austerity measures affected home life in just about every aspect. It was impossible to go shopping as it had been in peacetime. Obtaining basic items that were needed at home was difficult at best and more often than not unobtainable. While it was invariably mainly women who felt the lack of clothes, make-up and toiletries most keenly; everyone craved for plentiful food and other home comforts. After all, it was not just the luxuries that were scarce, but essentials as well, such as bedding, curtains, cutlery, crockery, light bulbs and even cleaning materials.

Only those who had been bombed out of their homes or newlyweds were allowed to buy new furniture. Second-hand furniture was almost as difficult to get as, like toys and wedding dresses, they were desirable commodities, snapped up by desperate buyers – and prices soared. In August 1944 *Good Housekeeping* ran an article called "Wartime Hope Chest". Written by Christine Palmer, it suggested ideas for those setting up home. One area focused on "Second-hand Furniture" and ran:

> "Second-hand furniture presents all kinds of exciting possibilities. Freed from ugly mouldings and clumsy handles,

it can be given new beauty by stripping and painting with flat white paint. Decorate, if you wish, with simple designs, using artists' colours and a good camel-hair brush. Victorian what-nots can be converted easily into bedside tables or dumb waiters. Ornate Victorian mirrors, which can often be bought for a song, stripped and painted white or any pastel colour, can be hung over a low table or shelf to make most attractive 'dressing tables'."

Other necessities such as mattresses, cots, alarm clocks, torches, glassware and saucepans were virtually impossible to find too. Jam jars were often used as drinking glasses; new parents were advised to make cots out of old drawers and in cafés, sugar spoons were attached to sugar bowls by string as cutlery was so difficult to replace. In 1942 restrictions became even more severe. If, on the rare occasion any necessary items were found in the shops, prices were usually extortionate. Flour sacks or butter muslin was used as curtains, bleached or dyed and ironed, gathered up to adorn windows between the blackout curtains and the room. Maisie Walker recalls:

"Hessian sacks that food was delivered in were begged from the grocers, to be washed and made into pegged rugs – the 'pile' made out of clothing that was long past its wearable state, after having the best cut out to see if something could be made out of it. All buttons were cut off and put in the button box that families used to have then. I inherited my mother's button box that still had buttons in it that had been removed from clothes that were no longer serviceable. Lavender bags were made to be put in the wardrobe to keep the clothes smelling fresh."

Sadie Belasco crocheted "lace" curtains out of thin string, rather like macramé. Each curtain had a fairly intricate matching pattern and she made one for every window in the house. Rug-making was another popular handicraft as carpets became ever more worn. In the book *101 Things to Do in Wartime*, instructions for making a rug were included. The chapter explained how to prepare the wool by winding it round a gauge and cutting it into strands of uniform length. The book also mentioned how "pile rugs" could be made with strips of felt or cuttings from old silk stockings. Pile rugs, also known as rag rugs were a means of using up all the scraps that might otherwise have been wasted. Eileen Watkins remembered:

> "My great-aunt used to cut leftover bits of fabric into strips, about one inch wide. Then with a hook, she pulled the strips through the holes in a sack. When she'd worked across the sack like this, she trimmed the pile to make it completely even and cut and hemmed round the edges of the sack. She made several of these lovely, colourful rugs, some small, some large and gave one to everyone in our family."

New life for old sheets

From October 1942 coupons were required to buy household linen, including sheets and towels, curtains and furnishing materials. It was particularly difficult for families with children. Household goods that could be bought were extremely basic, utility style. Towels were either grey or white and in three sizes. Sheets were only made in coarse cotton; no softer cotton or linen and certainly no colours. Most families made do with what they already had, but even items that were new in 1939 became worn and shabby by the middle of the war. In 1943 the Board of Trade issued an article in *Good Housekeeping*. Headed "New Life for Old Sheets", it showed various ways of making the most of household fabrics. The main image featured a woman tearing a sheet in half, with the words:

> "Watch for signs of wear and deal with a sheet that needs it before there's a hole. Tear or cut it in half lengthwise and join the selvedges in a flat seam by hand and then machine-hem the outer edges. These thin parts will go under the mattress where there's a little strain on them, so your re-made sheet is almost as strong as when new."

The piece continued with various tips, such as dealing with stains, how to make towels out of other household fabrics. At the bottom, a heading declared "Join a Make Do and Mend Class". It read:

"Sewing and household jobbery classes and mending parties are being formed all over the country. Already there are hundreds of them in full swing. Any Citizens' Advice Bureau will be glad to tell you where and when your nearest class or party meets, and how you can join or help to form one in your own district. *Mend and Make-do to save buying new.*"

Useful jobs that girls can do – to help win the war was published by the Board of Trade. It began: "Girls simply must be able to use their needles neatly in wartime – here are a few hints on sewing for beginners. But needlework isn't enough in these days when EVERYTHING must be made the most of; see if you can't turn your hand to other jobs round the house." It continued with step-by-step buttonhole making; mending lace or net curtains; making cushion covers; washing and ironing hints and even how to fix a loose knife handle. Another leaflet issued by the Board of Trade explained "Simple Household Repairs and how to handle them". It included instructions on repairing saucepans with holes in, patching a piece of carpet, fixing a frayed electricity flex or a loose hammer head, unblocking a sink, re-webbing a seat and patching damaged or dirty wallpaper, for example:

"When a papered wall is damaged, the paper can be patched so it is hardly noticeable. Remove the torn or stained bit where loose. Cut out a piece of wallpaper rather larger than that you have removed and tear the edge so that it is rough and irregular – this makes the patch inconspicuous. Paste on carefully."

Several people recall how they salvaged old bedding or towels:

"My mother patched a lot of our sheets, but when they became too worn; I helped her cut down doubles into singles and even singles into cot sheets."
"Very worn sheets were cut up, hemmed and used as tea towels or men's handkerchiefs."
"We cut large, worn towels into two smaller towels."
"I remember my aunt cutting up a worn tablecloth and making placemats and napkins with them instead."

In the "Wartime Hope Chest" from *Good Housekeeping*, further tips were given about enhancing plain sheets or towels:

"A series of French mottoes, for instance, cross-stitched along the borders in scarlet, makes a set of utility towels look very distinguished. Unrationed net and lace can be made into elegant table mats and frilled slip covers for small cushions."

Patchwork and appliqué

Magazine articles were full of ideas about putting odds and ends to good use. One article showed how to make a "shell" patchwork blanket using wool oddments. It ran:

"Short lengths of wool should never be thrown away, but should be tied together and wound into multi-coloured balls and kept on one side for making knitted blankets. These are excellent for children's cots and beds and indeed for adults' beds as well, although a too large expanse of wool tends to sag in wear unless it is very tightly knitted and the yarn is well-spun."

There followed a knitting pattern for a

"Shell" patchwork knitted blanket:
Using no.12 needles, cast on 41 stitches and knit about eight rows. Still working in garter stitch, knit two together each side of the centre stitch on alternate rows until three stitches remain. Knit these three stitches together and fasten off. When a good number of these "shells" have been made, sew them carefully together, beginning from the middle of the blanket so that the colours can be arranged in a pleasing pattern of light and dark shades. The blanket will be most effective with a border of "shells" in the same colour.

The book *101 Things to Do in Wartime* included a section on using patchwork to renovate worn, torn or tatty looking rooms. It began:

"Patchwork provides an excellent and economical way of putting to practical use all kinds of odds and ends of plain and coloured fabrics. Counterpanes, cushion covers, tablecloths and innumerable small articles, by the exercise of patience and a little ingenuity, can be made highly decorative. Harmonising of colours and the matching of patterns will help in forming treatments that will transform otherwise unused or useless scraps into original designs."

The invaluable little book went on to give detailed advice about patchwork designs and colour combinations:

"The simplest patchwork is formed by squares of material sewn together and finished with a plain border...The size of the squares will, of course, depend on the material available and also the size of the finished work...When a colour scheme has been evolved, the size of the square should be cut out in cardboard with allowance of a definite amount for turning in, and the material should be cut accurately to the template. In sewing up the squares it will be found simpler to sew the squares to form complete strips and then sew the strips together."

A section on appliqué followed the chapter on patchwork, which explained how lace, satin or felt appliquéd on different fabrics, in blanket stitch could enhance many household objects. Further ideas included applying lace shapes to a vellum lampshade or on the surface of a jam jar, finished with transparent varnish or brightening the insides of blackout curtains with brightly coloured flower or geometric shapes.

Many women tried to redecorate before their husbands came home on leave to make their homes more welcoming, but this was not easy. Household paint was in short supply and only came in brown, cream, green or white, so various ideas were tried, such as stippling one or two colours on a white or cream background, or stencilling below a dado or picture rail. Despite their best efforts however most homes looked drab and dilapidated, and as American servicemen began arriving from 1942 they were warned not to be shocked at the dreariness of British homes.

Wot, no cleaning materials?

As the war continued, along with other essentials, household cleaning materials disappeared off shop shelves. To meet the desperate pleas of readers, newspapers often featured readers' cleaning tips. Several people who were children during the war remembered using some of the ideas:

"My mother used scrunched-up newspaper for cleaning windows and mirrors. It worked brilliantly and I still use it today!"

"My grandmother sprinkled bicarbonate of soda on her carpet before brushing it about ten to fifteen minutes later. Any dog or food smells disappeared."

"A small jar of vinegar in the dining room absorbs unpleasant odours."

"Vinegar wiped on all kitchen surfaces with a soft, damp sponge or cloth leaves no smell and the kitchen will always be sparkling clean."

"My mum used washing soda to wash our clothes and then afterwards to clean the kitchen sink."

"There was none of the fancy cleaning gear about then like there is now. We used to put soda crystals in the washing up water and threw it in the sink with boiling water poured over it to dissolve any grease in the waste pipe and the same down the grates outside to stop them from smelling."

"Use bicarbonate of soda to scour shiny materials without scratching, such as aluminium, chrome, jewellery, porcelain, silver and tin."

"We poured a little bicarbonate of soda in an egg cup and put it in the larder, or sprinkled it in the bin, on carpets, armchairs and drains to eliminate smells and refresh everything."

"Shoe polish wasn't available so people were advised to cut a potato in half and use that to bring a shine to their shoes."

"Mother and I always put lemon juice in with our whites to whiten the wash."

"White vinegar makes a great fabric softener."

New uses for old stockings

Although stockings were so desirable to most women, even if they were obtained, they did not last and were often put to use when they could no longer be worn. Uses included:

Cutting them up to use for stuffing cushions, soft toys or for making rag rugs.

Cutting them into thin 'rings' and using them (like elastic bands) to hold greaseproof paper on jars of jam or other preserves.

Washed, dried and stretched over an embroidery ring, a piece of stocking worked well as a sieve!

Using them whole or cut up, old stockings made effective dusters – particularly good for polishing mirrors or glass.

Rose Campin observed: "Throughout the war everyone in Britain was philosophical. There was so much to worry about that you didn't make a fuss over things you couldn't prevent, you just got on with it and made do with what you could."

Christmas

Along with so many things, most traditional British celebrations disappeared during the war. Guy Fawkes' Night vanished first as gunpowder was needed for weapons and bonfires were in breach of blackout rules. Weddings and birthdays were reduced, but the one day that everyone still celebrated throughout the war was Christmas. As with most things to do with the home, it usually fell to women to organise.

When war was declared in September 1939 most people believed that it would be over by Christmas, but in the event, six Christmases passed before it ended. The government made a point that Christmases should be celebrated as closely as they could to those before the war to cheer everyone up and to help make things seem as "normal" as possible. Christmas of 1939, although just over two months into the conflict, was already different from anything experienced before. The blackout was newly imposed, higher taxes were being paid and families were broken up, with men away fighting and many children and others evacuated. Those caring for evacuees were also hard-pressed to make things seem "normal". Although there had been no air raids by that time, the authorities advised people not to bring back their evacuated children, but many did. Dutifully or perhaps more because they realised the importance of keeping a semblance of normality throughout the war, no matter what, Christmas became a day when everyone celebrated, no matter where they were, what they were doing, or what had happened. Everyone tried to forget their troubles and to focus on lifting the spirits. In 1940 (when many children were once again evacuated), *Woman and Home* magazine reported:

> "Christmas this year will, for most of us, have a deeper significance than ever before…the coloured paper caps which will go amusingly well with the unusual uniforms which many of us – women as well as men – may be wearing, and although the table may not groan so heavily as at other Christmases under the burden of good things on it, we may even get fun out of making the little less go a longer way – a sort of defiant good-humour and incorrigible happiness.'

This was the Dunkirk, Blitz or wartime spirit. Those with evacuees staying with them were given helpful advice on suitable forms of entertainment, with party games and food that they might enjoy. By the following year, the Blitz had started and the true horrors of war had taken hold. Approximately 24,000 civilians had been killed in the bombing. Sheila Dunne remembered it:

> "We were all poor, food was rationed, there was little good news and yet somehow, Christmas came and we felt obliged to celebrate. Food was rationed, sweets were scarce and our old, pre-war decorations appeared almost appeared like a mockery. If you thought about it, it seemed silly to celebrate, but on the other hand, what else were we to do?"

For the first couple of years at least, most people used the decorations they had before the war, but as these wore out or became damaged, many made decorations at home. There were no new decorations in the shops, with paper on ration and glass in short supply. Paper chains were the most common decoration to make. They were easy and cheap and they soon made any room look festive. Initially made out of colourful wrapping paper or even gummed strips of coloured paper, newspaper soon replaced this as paper became scarce. A paste was made out of flour (often soya or haricot bean flour as wheat flour was quite difficult to obtain) and water. Making decorations was a task often given to children as cutting, colouring, folding, looping and sticking strips of paper was a way of keeping them amused and occupied. Some made newspaper lanterns from rectangles of paper folded in half with slits cut across the fold. These were opened out, then curved round and glued together with a small paper handle glued on the top:

Christmas lanterns
Paper
Scissors
Sticky tape
Paste
Ruler
Pencil
Paint

1. Measure and mark a strip of paper, five inches by half an inch. Cut it out; it will be the lantern handle.
2. Measure and mark a paper rectangle, five inches by four inches. Cut this out. If you wish, decorate your lanterns with painted patterns.
3. Fold the rectangle in half lengthwise.
4. Measure and mark three inch straight lines on the rectangle, at right angles to the fold, half an inch apart, starting at one of the short edges and working across.
5. Cut on these marked lines across the fold and unfold the paper.
6. Re-crease the paper in the opposite direction. This will hide any pencil marks.
7. Curve your lantern around and paste the two matching shorter ends together.

8. Paste the handle to the top of the lantern.
Make as many lanterns as you wish and hang them on string across
a room.

Several ideas for home-made decorations were published in women's magazines. The "Daisy Chain" was one of these:

Daisy chain

[In card or paper,] cut out numerous small flower shapes about the
size of a shilling. Paint these in bright colours and then thread them
alternately on fine string or yarn with either bugle beads or chopped
hollow corn stalks. If you have neither of these, use coloured string
or wool and make a knot each side of the flower to keep it in place.

All kinds of items were used to make the home more festive. Egg shells and fir cones were painted and displayed on mantelpieces, while he silver paper from cheese spread was sometimes saved to be used on makeshift trees. Margaret Arthur recalled making paper chains:

"I loved making paper chains during the evenings in December with my sister. We cut strips out of old newspapers and glued them together with flour and water paste. When they were dry, we pinned them on each corner of the room, high up on the ceiling. We always made enough paper chains to stretch right across the room, crisscrossing in the middle. It kept us busy and we felt a great sense of achievement when we'd finished!"

Maisie Walker remembers her childhood Christmases:

"Newspaper was used to make Christmas trimmings. After being cut in strips and threaded through each other and being dabbed with a tiny bit of glue to make them stick, these paper chains were pinned across the ceilings with wool pompoms hanging in between. The pompoms were made by using the cardboard covers that used to cover bottles of milk. Two of these put together made nice sized woolly pompom because the middle of the cardboard could be pressed out without using scissors to cut it. Often any glittery jewellery was strung over the chains just to make it look a bit more festive. Unfortunately Christmas trees were not available during the war but we still did what we could to make the place look jolly. Children did not have expensive toys then but seemed content with an old sock of Dad's that had been filled up with an orange and an apple plus a few sweets and a comic or a drawing book and crayons. The highlight would be a brand new shining penny to spend that was found in the toe of the sock."

During the Blitz, for those in targeted locations, Christmas was celebrated in their shelters. Many recall the parties in the London Underground where strangers mingled with each other and parties overlapped. The feeling of camaraderie was never stronger. In at least one station a Christmas tree was put up with gifts on it for the children, some of whom dressed up in whatever costumes or finery their families could find for them. Various voluntary groups, including London Transport workers, members of the WVS and the Salvation Army, handed out sweets to the children and sold hot drinks, sandwiches and other snacks. The Salvation Army also sent out parties of carol singers to tour Underground stations on Christmas night, culminating in a large and charming concert in King's Cross station. In other shelters, people started their own carol singing groups, played games and ate picnics they had made beforehand. In the run up to Christmas newspapers and magazines had made plenty of suggestions about how people could celebrate the day, whether in a location that was being heavily bombed, or far away in the country. Either way, the hardships made things difficult. For those going into shelters, some rather unusual sandwich fillings were suggested, such as tinned tomatoes and Marmite, cream cheese and redcurrant jelly, or peanut butter with a savoury sauce. Amid a general feeling of making the day as special as possible, while accepting that it was different, *Good Housekeeping* published a recipe for a Shelter Christmas Cake:

"The Anderson Shelter is a byword with most of us now and makes an amusing and topical subject for a cake, especially if there are children in the family. Bake the cake mixture in an oblong mould or small bread tin and allow to cool, then cover each side with a layer of marzipan, cutting a small 'door' out of the front piece. Next, cut and fix a piece right over the top, marking corrugations with a skewer. Gather the trimmings and knead in enough cocoa to make the colour of earth and bank them up against the sides of the shelter. Finally, cover with a layer of snow made by melting six or eight marshmallows and pouring over. Leave a clearing in front of the 'shelter' for a path and sprinkle with finely chopped burnt almonds to imitate gravel."

It seems odd that at a time when everyone was trying to pretend things were normal and so many disliked the dark, damp shelters that the magazine recommended making a cake that looked like one. In 1945, several months after the war ended, but rationing continued, the Ministry of Food published an article in *Good Housekeeping* entitled "Festive Fare for Christmas". It began:

"Don't you feel you and the family have earned the right to a little festivity this Christmas? To make the Christmas pudding, the Christmas cake and other seasonable things a little nearer to your memories of what such goodies should be? Well, the Ministry of Food has issued a leaflet containing some delightful suggestions and recipes."

The article continued with a few sample recipes, such as:

Macaroons
1 tablespoon water
1 oz margarine
1 teaspoon ratafia or almond essence
2 oz sugar
2 oz soya flour
Melt the margarine in the water; add the essence and sugar, then the soya flour. Turn on to a board and knead well. Roll mixture into balls, flatten slightly and bake in a moderate oven for 20 minutes till golden brown.

The Ministry of Food also published advertisements in newspapers and magazines. One was called "Christmas Fancies" that suggested two recipes to "fill the children's stockings". These were gingerbread men and honeycomb toffee.

Gingerbread Men
2 oz sugar or syrup
2 oz margarine
8 oz plain flour
½ level teaspoon mixed spice
2 level teaspoons ginger
Lemon substitute
1 level teaspoon bicarbonate of soda
Melt the syrup or sugar and margarine. Pour into a bowl. Add some flour and the spice and lemon substitute. Stir well. Dissolve the bicarbonate of soda in a tablespoon of tepid water and add to the mixture. Continue stirring, gradually adding more flour. Finish the process by turning out the mixture on to a well-floured board. Knead in the remainder of the flour. Roll a small ball for the head, flatten it and place it on the baking tin. Roll an oblong for the body and strips for the arms and legs. Join these together with a little reconstituted egg and put currants for the eyes.

As each year passed the war made Christmas more difficult. Cards became smaller, less extravagant and printed on flimsy paper rather than card; wrapping paper and labels were hard to find and Christmas trees were in short supply. Those that were sold were expensive and were usually chopped down parts of larger trees. People became quite inventive, making their own "Christmas trees" out of tinsel and wire, cardboard, twigs painted white or small bushes or trees dug up from the garden and replaced after the event. In 1942 an article in the *Radio Times* announced: "Christmas trees are scarce and very expensive, and imitation ones prohibitive in price, so a few carefully cherished flowers or small sprays of holly will, I expect, provide the Christmas decorations in most homes." But many families were not content with making do in this way and tales of creativity are rife. Some recall bending wire coat hangers or chicken wire, covering these in paper or cotton wool and decorating them with small lights or small objects. These were usually put in windows to be seen from without before the blackout and from within to brighten the home during the long evenings. Shapes for these makeshift decorations ranged from snowmen, to trees, to large stars. Janet Simpson remembered collecting old, finished light bulbs and painting them with silver and gold paint, then tying them with thread and hanging them on their wire and paper tree which they had painted green. "We stuck coloured stars on the tree and made tiny 'presents' out of empty matchboxes and hung those on too."

As ever, magazines were full of creative ideas. *Stitchcraft* was published from 1932 to 1982 for "needlewomen". It began essentially to market branded wools, but it continued to be published for 50 years and moved on from its initial purpose. Although popular and helpful during the war years, it was difficult to keep filled with ideas, as many types of wool, yarns, fabrics, threads and trimmings that were needed to create most stitched or knitted items became unobtainable. The magazine shrank to half its original size, was printed on insubstantial paper and sometimes covered two months at a time. Yet it continued to try to appeal to readers and in 1941, it published various ideas and instructions for making Christmas toys and decorations. It began:

> "There will be very few toys in the shops this Christmas, but there is no reason why you should not have plenty on the family tree, provided you are ready to spend a little time and thought on making them. Here are several ideas which those who are quick-fingered will be able to make quite easily…You need brightly coloured enamel paints in as many colours as you can find; glue; small pieces of stout paper or thin cardboard; and plenty of space to work in, as you are going to make a glorious mess."

The editorial continued with instructions for making a Christmas tree:

> "Roll a tube of thick paper, any colour…The ends, snipped down for two inches, are bent outwardly for the base and inwardly for the tip later on. Glue firmly in position along the long edge and paint in any bright colour. Now make different

sized squares of paper, the largest 15 inches square, and the smallest six inches square. Roll these into cone shapes, glue in position and paint green. When dry, fix to trunk with fine twine or linen thread. Use a sharp needle that will pass through the tube easily without bending it out of shape. Cover the main trunk in this way, the small cones at the top and the large ones at the bottom, working up from the base. Paint a few white or silver spots here and there on the cones, or, if you have any silver frost, stick on some of that instead. Finish off the top by gluing together the slits at one end very firmly so that they form a point to be gathered together at the top by a big ribbon bow."

Although they had remained popular tree decorations before the war, candles were rarely used during the war, partly because of the fire hazard and partly because everyone held on to their candles in case bombings caused electricity failures. Eric Brown recalled making a simple circuit of coloured fairy lights he found from before the war and connecting the two end wires to his bicycle lamp battery. His parents used this to illuminate their tree (a branch cut from a tree in the garden and painted white) for the duration of the war. Other decoration ideas included making a strong solution of Epsom salts and painting this on to holly leaves or dipping the leaves into the mixture. When it dried, the white salts sparkled like frost. Jean Pink made her own wrapping paper and labels with potato prints on newspaper.

Christmas 1943 saw shortages at their height but magazines continued to offer creative and enterprising methods for making decorations and presents, such as knitted slippers, scarves and gloves, brooches made from scraps of wool, felt or buttons, and embroidered bookmarks and calendars. Most people made their own crackers, using more old newspapers and string, filling them with tiny items like hairclips, sweets, marbles or even small coins. Pat Parsons, who was 10 when the war broke out, remembered what happened in her house:

"My mother used to keep a 'Christmas box'. All through the year she'd collect bits and pieces and put them in the box. So many things went into that box; thimbles, bits of paper, ribbons, hard-to-come-by sweet wrappers or even sweets themselves, scraps of fabric, string and buttons, for example, and at the end of the year, we opened the box and used the things in there. Things like thimbles, hair clips, pretty buttons, tin whistles or sweets went into our homemade crackers, which we made from newspaper and string. There were no bangs in our crackers – we'd had enough of bangs during air raids!"

Peggy Johnson, who was six when the war began, lived in East Anglia. She remembered:

"By bartering I think, my grandfather usually managed to get us a small Christmas tree which we decorated with our pre-war decorations. These were carefully wrapped up each year in newspaper and kept in a box in a cupboard. I spent hours making paper chains out of newspaper which I painted with my small box of paints and I was allowed to use a tiny bit of flour to make paste to glue the strips together. I made our Christmas cards too – out of small pieces of paper or card. Father Christmas would leave me a stocking containing a piece of fruit, a sixpence, sometimes a pencil, hankies or something knitted, like a scarf or mittens."

Even before the war Christmases were not extravagant celebrations and presents for most were modest, but as things became ever more stringent, it was extremely difficult for families to find gifts for each other. Most presents were practical; seeds, gardening tools, bottled fruit, books or bath salts for example. The most popular present in 1940 was soap. Fewer toys were available and people began selling second-hand toys and games, often at extortionate prices. Many people made toys, some following the instructions in newspapers and magazines, for things such as rag dolls and glove puppets or knitted animals made from old worn clothes or dolls' houses, sweetshops or post offices, made from old packets and cartons. Audrey Thorpe recalled: "The only toys I remember getting at Christmases during the war were knitted ones! Knitted dolls, a clown, a rabbit and a lion – I think my mum made most of them, but she might have been helped by my Auntie Maureen!"

Treats

In 1944, the last Christmas of the war, the Ministry of Food announced that it would be giving everyone extra treats that year. These included an extra one and a half pounds of sugar, eight (old) pennies' worth of meat and half a pound of sweets. In one of the many ideas for homemade gifts that year, an article in *Woman's Weekly* proposed a personally decorated box of matches:

> "...A box of matches makes a very welcome gift. If you want to make this more important-looking, dress the box up by sticking a scrap of pretty wallpaper, or decorative Christmas paper at the front and back of it. Should you have more than one box to give away, a packet of one or two, decorated differently and tied with a ribbon, makes the present something other than mere matches."

9
OUTSIDE THE HOME

"The nation is united when danger looms in sight; we march along together and sing with all our might." ~ From *We must all stick together* written by Ralph Butler and R. Wallace in 1939

Before the war, approximately 19 million people in Britain went to the cinema each week. By 1945, despite about 330 cinemas having been destroyed by bombs, the number of cinema-goers had risen to 30 million and box office takings had doubled. From 4th September 1939, British cinema was governed by the Ministry of Information. Responsible for publicity and propaganda throughout the war, the Ministry aimed to "present the national case to the public at home and abroad". It recognised the importance of the cinema in maintaining morale and maintained close contact with film-makers in Britain. Yet it was Hollywood films that were the most popular with the public, such as *Gone with the Wind, Casablanca, Citizen Kane, Brief Encounter* and *Henry V*, as they were colourful and glamorous, while British films were more focused on depicting the courage of the Forces in action. These were popular, but not as escapist as the American films. Top British stars of the time included Vivien Leigh, Laurence Olivier, James Mason and Margaret Lockwood, while Hollywood stars that kept everyone flocking in included Errol Flynn, Humphrey Bogart, Ingrid Bergman, Clark Gable, Bette Davis, Charlie Chaplin, Betty Grable, Rita Hayworth and Veronica Lake. During the early years of the war, when Britain was facing the possibility of invasion and defeat by the Nazis and America was remaining detached from the war, the MGM producer Sidney Franklin made a film as a tribute to Britain at war. *Mrs Miniver* was the story of a middle-class English family in the Blitz, starring Greer Garson. Without a single battle scene in the film, the sentimental portrayal of the hardships endured and surmounted by the British family inspired derision and contempt from British film-goers, but great sympathy among the Americans and as a result, American support for involvement in the war increased significantly. Winston Churchill described the film as "propaganda worth 100 battleships".

Shops and shopping

Cinema, dances, theatre and other forms of entertainment were imperative in keeping up people's spirits. But they were only a means of escapism as everyone continued to face immense difficulties every day through the shortages, dangers (for those in areas that were bombed) and anxieties of separation and the safety of loved-ones far away. While many previously house-proud individuals had to leave their dirty clothes and dishes piling up, could not renovate their houses, and could only bath once a week, many others found the strain of putting an appetising meal on the table each day was even more testing. On top of this, whatever they did outside the home, whether in voluntary services, war work or anything else, everyone had to queue. In many towns, queuing was unavoidable, whether it was for food, buses, trains, or even cinemas, and without supermarkets or fridges, housewives often had to queue at several shops every day. In the main towns and cities, they waited patiently in line outside butchers', bakers', grocers' and greengrocers' often for hours at a time, frequently to discover that when they reached the counter, that whatever it was they had been queuing for had sold out. Others refused to queue. Peggy Milroy who lived in West London for a large part of the war remembers:

> "Everyone queued – everywhere! For shoes, newspapers, toiletries, for – you name it, we queued. But it was always done politely; we accepted that we were all in the same boat."

In smaller towns and villages, the shopkeepers ensured that everyone received their allocated share. Barbara Matthews, who lived in Hertfordshire, remembered:

> "In my experience there was no queuing for rationed food because you always got your proper share with no trouble in the course of normal shopping. The only queuing was when people heard that something unusual (like a cargo of bananas) had arrived and then it was first come first served. The shopkeepers gave a set, reasonable amount to each customer. Not huge amounts. We never bothered with queuing for unusual things; we just lived on our rations and what we raised in our back garden. We thought people queuing for a few biscuits or sweets (before they were rationed at the end of the war) were silly."

With no new produce to display on shelves and in windows, shopkeepers often used empty crates or boxes, or plaster models of the items that they previously had in abundance. To avoid any uncomfortable scenes, empty cartons and packets used like this for display were often labelled "empty packet, for display purposes only". Rationed food could only be bought where housewives had registered, so if they worked, they had to queue during their lunch breaks or after work in the blackout. Queuing in the blackness was not pleasant, but in their desperation to keep their families fed and home lives as "normal" as possible, queuing became a routine. Many women were known to queue wherever they saw a line forming, only asking what they were queuing for once they were standing there. Queuing became such an integral aspect of life that in 1942, the Minister of War Transport issued a "Statutory Rule and Order" on the subject. It included:

> "…Where no barrier rail is provided, any six or more persons…waiting…shall form and keep a queue or line of not more than two abreast on the footway.
> A person shall not take or endeavour to take any position in a queue or line formed…other than behind the persons already forming the same…"

Nevertheless, no matter how desperate they were, there was still the feeling of general supportiveness for each other, as Barbara Matthews recollects:

"There was a strong feeling that we must all share the food available fairly and that having money should not give you an advantage. Rationing was a lot of work for the shopkeepers, but it did work and nearly everyone was satisfied we were all treated equally."

The other side of the counter

Among many concerns, not least obtaining goods to sell, making sure that fair trading was practised and trying to keep their regular customers happy, shopkeepers were hard-pressed to keep things going. There was little passing or new trade, especially if they sold predominantly rationed goods, as shoppers had to register with individual shops and few new products were being manufactured. The paper shortage meant that there were no bags – shoppers either dutifully brought their own with them, took old newspapers to wrap goods in, or they managed without. Sunday evenings were when many shopkeepers did their weekly coupon counting. Usually this involved other members of the family as it was so fiddly and time-consuming. Sweet coupons were the worst for shopkeepers to deal with. Hundreds of bits of paper had to be collected, counted and noted on a form, for which the Food Office issued a voucher for further orders of stock from the wholesaler. Any errors in the counting created real problems. If they claimed too few, shopkeepers did not receive their full entitlement of new supplies, and if they claimed too many, they were likely receive a fine or summons to court. Then there were the major, daily problems of giving each customer a fair entitlement. Too much bone in a meat ration and the customer would probably complain; even slightly overly generous portions and the shopkeeper would run out of supplies and not be able to provide all with their allowances that week. Many shopkeepers and shop assistants recall being singled-out by wealthier customers, through gifts and invitations to tea, in attempts to coax a few "extras" out of them. This crossing of the class barriers would never have happened before the war, but as soon as the war was over, the enticements and unexpected friendliness ceased.

As a consequence of having fewer goods to sell, most shops shortened their opening hours. In October 1939 the Home Secretary made it a rule that all shops, except tobacconists, closed by 6pm with one later night allowed per week. By 1941 shop opening hours were reduced still further. Most large stores across the country closed at 4pm for the rest of the war, while factories lengthened their working hours. Restaurateurs struggled as much as everyone else. They had to ensure that the food was worthy of the effort of going out to eat and paying for it – no easy feat during rationing. But eating out at restaurants, canteens, cafés and British Restaurants increased during the war as eating out was not rationed. The government provided advice for those running factory canteens, which were also expanded during the war. *Canteen Catering* was a pamphlet issued by the Ministry of Food. Along with recipes, quantities and other helpful suggestions, it recommended canteen managers introduce unfamiliar foods gradually, such as oatmeal and different recipes for canteens in Scotland and England to meet varied tastes common to each part of the country, such as Cornish pasties or black pudding.

Apart from factory canteens, which were helped by the government, customers could buy restaurant meals off-ration, but it was still difficult for restaurant owners to obtain food and the government imposed fairly rigorous rules. After 1942, when no restaurant could charge more than five shillings a meal and only three courses could be served, with one of them counting as a 'main' course, things became even more controlled. Many a restaurateur however made more money by charging for wine, bread and other "extras". The government provided advice for those running canteens and with so many cookery books about, the focus was on eating healthily within the restrictions and within a short time, many restaurateurs became experts in providing nutritious and appetising meals, rather than anything complex or fancy, and everyone paid more attention to nutritious values and value for money than they had previously. All restaurants, canteens and cafés had to grow their own food as did private homes and the healthy, plain fare that was served was seen as helping with the war effort. Many restaurants displayed the sign: "Victory 'V' meals", which signified that eating the healthy food provided within would help keep you healthy and so ultimately would help Britain win the war. British Restaurants, that were set up by the Ministry of Food and run by local councils on a non-profit making basis, were usually even cheaper than other restaurants, with a three-course meal invariably costing no more than 9d. Standards varied, but the good ones were extremely popular with large numbers of regulars. Run by local authorities, British Restaurants evolved from the London County Council's "Londoners' Meals Service" which began in September 1940 as a temporary, emergency system for feeding those who had been bombed out of their homes and to provide school meals for non-evacuated children in need of them. From 1941 it had assumed the additional responsibility for canteens at ambulance and civil defence establishments. British Restaurants were open to all but mainly served office, ambulance and industrial workers. The restaurants themselves were often run by women who were used to cooking for their families. Winston Churchill is said to have suggested the name "British Restaurants" to inspire feelings of patriotism – and it was preferred to the original and somewhat unpalatable earlier name given to them of "Community Feeding Centres". One of the many benefits of British Restaurants was that even if a person had run out of – or lost – their rations, they could still afford to eat. Particularly popular in London, by the summer of 1941, there were over 200 British Restaurants in the LCC area and by the end of 1943, there were over 2,000 nationwide.

The Rural Pie Scheme
Food eaten outside the home stimulated plenty of enterprising initiatives. Following the government's requests, in late 1941, WVS workers provided field workers at harvest time with daily hot meat pies. By the end of the year, over 70,000 pies were cooked and distributed to farm workers. Two years later, because of popularity of the scheme, the government directed each county to establish a special committee to administer and control their own production of pies. The pies were soon sold extremely cheaply, on a non-profit making basis, to anyone who worked away from the convenience of

canteens or British Restaurants. The scheme continued to grow rapidly, and by 1943 there was a weekly delivery of more than 120,000 hot pies across the country, with a further 36,000 during harvest times or hop-picking. The pies were distributed by rail and then by any other means possible.

The government provided advice for those running factory canteens, which were also expanded during the war. "Canteen Catering" was a pamphlet issued by the Ministry of Food, asking managers to introduce familiar foods gradually.

Advice centres

In accordance with the Ministry of Information's primary task, to keep people informed and educated throughout the war, various advice centres were established along with all the leaflets and advertising. In 1938, in anticipation of a war, the National Council for Social Service (NCSS) had called a meeting where plans were drawn up to establish "Citizens Advice Bureaux" in the event of war. The following year, four days after the war broke out, the first 200 of these opened. Run entirely voluntarily by respected members of the community such as local bank managers, and funded by local councils, these government departments opened in various improvised offices, including cafés, church halls, private houses and even air raid shelters. One mobile unit even operated from a converted horsebox and travelled about heavily bombed areas to assist and advise those who were particularly adversely affected. By 1942 there were 1,074 Citizens Advice Bureaux across Britain. Each was established as an emergency service, to provide free, confidential, impartial and independent advice on a wide range of issues that were affecting the people of the local community. They were invaluable resources for all sorts of crises and problems experienced across society and helped to make communities feel that the authorities were supporting them. Problems included debt, damaged or destroyed homes and repairs, loss of ration books, tracing missing servicemen or prisoners of war, pensions, income tax, jobs and evacuation. Even family issues were brought to the CAB, as it became known. CAB advisors also worked with other voluntary services such as the Red Cross.

Health

Barbara Matthews recalls: "One of my abiding memories of the war years was of everyone becoming tireder and paler and more lined as the months and years went by. But in those days, no one had the modern problem of getting fat!"

Of course they did have the problem of getting ill – and of not being able to afford a visit to the doctor. Visiting one's GP was neither as convenient nor as straightforward during the war as it became after the NHS was introduced in 1948. Before that, patients usually had to pay for their healthcare. Free treatment was sometimes available from some teaching or charity hospitals, such as the Royal Free Hospital in London. After April 1930 the London County Council took responsibility for 140 hospitals, medical schools and other similar institutions to try to provide health treatment for all Londoners. By the time war broke out nine years later the LCC was running the largest public health service in Britain. There were private health insurance schemes, often organised by companies and paid for by those in regular employment. Employees had a small sum deducted from their weekly wages, to which their employers and the government added contributions. But this was only taken up by certain trades and occupations. Other insurances were sought and paid for by individuals and families and while some of these contributory schemes were small and unreliable, many developed to become large, trustworthy and well-established. One of the largest was the Hospital Saving Association (HSA), which in 1939 had about two million members. The HSA required a contribution from its members for about 4d per person per week, which helped towards the cost of visiting the doctor or hospital. Certain common or deadly illnesses such as tuberculosis were not covered by these insurances, and medicines were paid for separately, but health insurance was considered a necessity by many. Qualified pharmacists were called up to the armed forces later than the general population because of the importance of their civilian work. But on the whole, most people stayed away from doctors if possible and treated themselves to defend against illness. Being healthy was a vital part of the war effort. Everyone was needed to work at their optimum capacity, as time taken off was a drain on all resources. The government recommended fresh air and exercise whenever possible, advising on weekend cycling tours or hiking breaks. As one advertisement for Ovaltine declared:

"Health and Efficiency must be Maintained!
Never before has it been so urgent a duty for everyone to maintain the health, energy and the will-to-win which are so vital to the success of the national effort."

The BBC introduced *The Daily Dozen* and *Up in the Morning Early*; 20 minute radio programmes featuring 10 minutes of exercises for men and 10 minutes of exercises for women. From 1942 *The Radio Doctor* was another daily programme, this time of five minutes duration, with Dr Charles Hill giving tips on how to keep well, what foods to eat to supplement rations healthily and quick remedies for specific ailments. Many recall his insistent sign-off line: "Make sure the bowels are well open!" With the introduction of the Vitamin Welfare Scheme, which came into effect at the beginning of 1942, all children under two received free supplies of cod liver oil and blackcurrant juice or when available, orange juice. A year later, this was extended to include pregnant women and children under the age of five, who also, since 1940, had been provided with free milk under the National Milk Scheme, if the household had an income of less than 40 shillings a week. The 1944 Education Act made it an entitlement for children of poorer families to receive free school meals and for all children in the United Kingdom under the age of 18 to receive one third of a pint of milk a day. Meanwhile, mothers dosed their children regularly with spoonfuls of malt, castor oil, liquid paraffin or syrup of figs, in efforts to ensure their good health. Maisie Walker remembers some of the popular remedies that were available (some more effective than others), such as Friars Balsam taken for coughs; an all-round antiseptic balm called Zam-Buk and an ointment called Wintergreen for aches, pains and cold symptoms; and Indian Brandee, taken for colic or female monthly pains. Yet these over-the-counter remedies were fairly limited, so many relied on homemade treatments. Bread or kaolin poultices were made to treat infected cuts or boils; the herb feverfew was steeped in hot water and sipped to subdue or avert headaches, solutions of cold tea were used to bathe swollen eyes, oil of cloves applied on cotton wool and held on a painful tooth helped to relieve toothache, a small warm onion or large boiled potato wrapped in a piece of flannel or a hot water bottle held against the ear were various treatments for earache. Bruises were smeared with a small lump of butter or olive oil or even a mustard poultice, potassium permanganate crystals were dissolved in varying solutions of water to cure athlete's foot, psoriasis or to take the irritation out of the chicken pox rash. Kitty Pink remembered: "If anyone was stung by a bee, we made a paste of bicarbonate of soda. It took the pain away instantly! White vinegar was used to neutralise wasp stings." The Ministry of Food paid people 3d per pound for rose-hips picked from the hedgerows, to make rose-hip syrup, which was extremely rich in vitamin C. As well as selling their own syrups – made by local branches of the WVS – the Ministry of Food issued a recipe for it:

Rose-hip Syrup
Ingredients
2 lbs rose-hips
4½ pts water
1¼ lb sugar
Method
Boil three pints water.
Mince hips coarsely and immerse immediately in the water.
Bring back to the boil and then leave to cool for fifteen minutes.
Pour into a flannel, muslin, or clean stocking and allow the liquid to drip through into a basin.
Return this residue to the saucepan, add another 1½ pints boiling water, stir and allow to stand for ten minutes.
Pour back into the jelly bag and allow to drip through into a basin.
To make sure all the hairs are removed from the rose-hips, pour through the muslin, flannel or stocking and allow the liquid to drip through again.
Put the juice into a clean saucepan and boil down until it measures about 1½ pints and then add 1¼ lb of sugar and boil for a further five minutes.
Pour into hot sterile bottles and seal at once.

Tip: It is advisable to use small bottles as the syrup will not keep for more than a week or two once the bottle is opened. Store in a dark cupboard.

The war saw the spread of blood transfusions, which were relatively new forms of treatment. Blood had been transferred between people for some time, but the keeping of blood stores had not. Statistics were not conclusive, but it is believed that nationwide, between 7th September 1940 and 16th May 1941, 41,000 civilians were killed and 137,000 injured during air raids. As a result of new techniques in blood storage mobile blood transfusion units were set up that travelled around towns and cities collecting blood to store and to use to save lives. Penicillin became used for treating both wounds and venereal diseases, although most medical developments like this were concentrated on care for the troops, with less impact on civilian medicine. More civilians trained as voluntary first aid assistants, learning to diagnose, treat and prevent minor illnesses and to treat injuries. First aid parties were formed, which involved groups of volunteers, trained by the British Red Cross, the St Andrew's Ambulance Corps and the St John Ambulance Brigade, or by local councils. First aid parties went directly to sites of new bombing and dealt with minor casualties on the spot, helping to ease the strain on the hospitals. Some members of the first aid parties helped as stretcher bearers, taking casualties to ambulances, first aid posts or hospitals. First aid posts cared for the victims of air raids and blackout accidents (of which there were many) usually for those who were well enough to return home, so every first aid post had at least one trained medical officer or doctor and one trained nurse. First aid posts were usually set up in specially adapted buildings, air raid shelters or Underground stations while some operated from mobile units. Some Boots stores were also used as first aid posts. Casualties going to first aid posts moved through three different sections: one where they were received and their problem assessed; a second for receiving treatment and a third where they could rest before being sent home or to hospital. One particular consequence of the Blitz was infection caused by the close proximity of so many people in confined communal shelters, and coughs caused by the damp. First aid posts were often inundated with sufferers of these debilitating infections. During the Blitz, several companies produced "ARP first aid kits" to help civilians cope with minor injuries. Used by Air Raid Wardens and families, they usually contained plasters, triangular bandages, gauze bandages, anti-gas ointment, sterilised dressings, an alcoholic solution of iodine, cotton wool, safety pins, splints, smelling salts (sal volatile), eye drops and a small first aid instruction book. In *101 Things to Do in Wartime* advice on treating wounds, shock and burns was given:

Wounds
"First aid for wounds consists in stopping the bleeding and in keeping the wound clean, using an antiseptic fluid, either a good proprietary brand or permanganate of potash dissolved in clean water..."

Shock
"The treatment for shock should be carried out apart from any treatment for injury... The patient should be placed on the floor, on a bed or couch, and laid flat. Clothing should be loosened at the neck, chest and waist, to allow room for breathing. The patient should be covered with a rug and hot-water bottles placed at the feet and when able to drink, and on no account before, give hot drinks or, in summer, cold water..."

Burns
"The treatment for burns is to remove any clothing that does not adhere to the burn and keep away the air until the burn is dressed. Scalds and burns on which the skin has not been broken can be covered with tannic acid jelly. If the patient has been overcome by smoke and fumes, breathing can be restored by artificial respiration, but this should not be attempted without previous training."

101 Things to Do in Wartime also gave useful advice about making and using various bandages and splints, including roller and triangular bandages and hand and finger bandaging. With so many opportunities and guidance, there was no excuse for anyone to be ignorant of basic first aid.

Entertainment

In spite of the crushing problems that people faced, literature and the arts flourished in Britain during the war. Escapism in many forms was welcomed to alleviate anxiety and despair, so reading; listening to music; art appreciation and theatre- and concert-going all became particularly popular. Although many writers and artists served in the Forces, some were employed by the Ministry of Information which set up the CEMA and the War Artists' Advisory Committee in an effort to enthuse the public with cultural events and concerts. CEMA was founded a few months after the outbreak of the war, divided into three departments of music, art and drama. The initial, immediate, problems it faced were in providing music and drama during the blackout, especially in areas that had suddenly been heavily populated with workers. One of the CEMA's initiatives was to set up touring companies presenting plays, concerts, art exhibitions, operas and ballets. And one of the most successful of these was the theatre productions that toured Royal Ordnance Factory Hostels around the country. Royal Ordnance Factories were government-run munitions factories. Established in relatively safe areas of the country, most of these were more or less self-contained, with generators, workshops, hostels, canteens, laundries and medical centres for the workers. The CEMA ROH tours proved exceptionally successful in boosting the workers' morale. Considering that many of these workers had little previous experience with the arts, it was both daring and innovative to stage plays by George Bernard Shaw, William Shakespeare, Somerset Maugham, Henrik Ibsen, Anton Chekov and others, but the response was overwhelmingly appreciative. Throughout the war, CEMA initiated many other successful endeavours and collaborations, often setting up entertainments and makeshift theatres in community or church halls. A CEMA report of 1944, *The Arts in Wartime*, stated: "It is a special aim of the Council to encourage the dispersal of the arts to centres which, mainly for reasons connected with the war, are cut off from enjoying them." With so many theatre hands in the Forces or employed in essential war work, initially keeping theatres open and viable during the war was believed to be an almost impossible task. When stage costumes and make-up were rationed and air raids disrupted performances, the difficulties seemed almost insurmountable. But it was soon realised that theatre was an outstandingly effective morale booster so CEMA and theatre owners tried new tactics. For a start, theatres in vulnerable areas ran performances in the late afternoons or early evenings rather than at night. If an air raid occurred during a performance, signs illuminated in the auditorium, informing audiences that an air raid was in progress and they were free to leave quietly for a shelter if they wished. Towards the end of the war, most chose to stay where they were and watch the play or show to the end.

Reading also surged in popularity. Books were taken into shelters, read on the usually delayed public transport journeys, or during long evenings in the blackout. In 1942 the Publishers' Association negotiated a *Book Production War Economy Agreement* designed to save paper while maintaining design. In 1943 publishers were allowed only a small percentage of their pre-war paper (a meagre 25 per cent of previous supplies, rising to just 42 per cent after the trade protested to the government). To try to match the demand amid such stringent reductions, books were produced on thinner paper with narrower margins and lighter bindings. Chapters often ran straight on from each other rather than starting on a new page. Penguin Books' innovative cheap paperbacks had been available since the early 1930s, and many other publishers struggled to maintain business as usual and most managed to produce legible, economical books. Public and subscription libraries like Boots and W. H. Smith were particularly popular and, in 1941, W. H. Smith introduced travelling bookstalls to replace established bookstalls that had been bombed. Most substantial towns had a Boots Booklovers Library and by 1939 there were 450 of these across Britain, supporting over half a million subscribers who were charged a small fee per book. Subscription libraries were valued in rural areas where no public lending library was provided by the local council. Reading matter varied, but the general trend was for gripping stories that provided plenty of escapism. Surprisingly perhaps, crime stories were just as popular as in less violent times. Although contemporary novels were enjoyed by many, by authors such as A. J. Cronin, Daphne du

Maurier, Agatha Christie, Monica Dickens, Frances Parkinson Keyes, James Thurber and Elizabeth Goudge, classics by authors such as Jane Austen, Charles Dickens and Anthony Trollope experienced a resurgence in popularity as people sought to immerse themselves in the relative comfort and safety of the past. Magazines, although reduced in size, were also enjoyed by many, with a diverse range available, including *Good Housekeeping*, *Punch*, *Picture Post*, *Lilliput*, *Woman's Weekly*, *Woman and Home*, *Country Life*, *The Listener*, *Fortnightly Review* and others. Containing relevant and topical information and guidance, they aroused feelings of community spirit, featuring heartening stories, ideas for improving day-to-day lives and often additional helpful advice from the government.

Art and advertising

When the War Artists Advisory Committee (WAAC) was formed in 1939 it aimed to direct and commission art to serve the war effort; through recording the conflict visually, raising morale and promoting national culture. Some of the most avant-garde artists in Britain were commissioned, including Percy Wyndham Lewis, C.R.W. Nevinson, John Piper, Graham Sutherland, Henry Moore and Stanley Spencer. Based in Britain, these particular artists' expressive and powerful evocations reinterpreted and reflected the difficulties shared on the Home Front.

At the beginning of the war, commercial artists suffered when the advertising industry effectively collapsed. In the light of more immediate concerns, advertising goods and services was perceived as an irrelevant luxury. It was soon realised however how important advertising, that notified and updated the public, actually was and many of the copywriters, graphic designers, typographers, illustrators, art directors and account executives who had worked in the advertising industry before the war were employed by the government. In their efforts to condense and convey information and messages to anxious, busy people who were struggling through adversity, these advertising specialists created some exceptionally unique, succinct and effective advertising campaigns.

160

A special job of work

Edwin J. Embleton had worked for 15 years for a publishing house when war broke out and he was almost immediately employed by the Ministry of Information. Within a short time he was working as art director and studio manager, employing painters, designers, illustrators, layout artists, typographers, calligraphers, cartoonists and more, effectively creating an advertising agency within the MoI. His remit was to produce all official government literature for both the general and overseas production divisions, and was responsible for preparing, overseeing and following all projects through to completion. His undertakings were huge, but at the end of the war, Churchill wrote a letter of thanks for his "special job of work" and awarded him the MBE (Member of the Order of the British Empire) for his services to the war effort.

The war forced everyone to be economical and there was no exception for commercial artists, who concisely captured and epitomised the atmosphere of the era with simple slogans and stylish images. Some of the most successful were: John Gilroy, Frank Newbould, Leslie Illingworth, Harold Forster, Pat Keely and Bert Thomas. Gilroy had been famous for his Guinness advertisements, but throughout the war he was employed by Embleton for the MoI. Illingworth became recognised for his political cartoons in the *Daily Mail* and *Punch* and a series of humorous posters for the Ministry of War Transport. Forster originally designed chocolate boxes, but among others, created the glamorous poster "Keep Mum – She's Not So Dumb" as part of the "Careless Talk Costs Lives" campaign. Keely meanwhile, designed the famous poster "Look Out in the Blackout!" There were many other commercial artists, all working behind the scenes, and all effectively helping to bolster the public's spirits with their crisp and creative ideas.

The monarchy

One of the biggest boosts to the collective morale was the attitude of the King and Queen, who remained at Buckingham Palace throughout the war, although they sent their daughters, Princesses Elizabeth and Margaret to Windsor Castle for safety. During the Blitz, Buckingham Palace suffered nine direct hits and after one of these when the royals toured some of the bombed areas of London, Queen Elizabeth famously declared: "It makes me feel I can look the East End in the face." The King also visited his troops in France and North Africa and founded the George Medal and the George Cross to honour the "many acts of heroism performed both by male and female persons especially during the present war." So the monarchy proved to have a hugely positive effect on the entire nation. The appearance of the royal couple among others living through the war at home, with their insistence that they would never leave Britain, increased the collective feeling that everyone was in the conflict together.

10
AFTERMATH

"Tomorrow, just you wait and see, there'll be love and laughter and peace ever after, tomorrow, when the world is free." ~ From *The White Cliffs of Dover*, written by Nat Burton, music by Walter Kent, first published in 1941

By the middle of 1944 Germany was clearly losing the war and everyone felt that the end was in sight. Although exhausted, a wave of optimism swept Britain and people relaxed a little. Then Hitler launched his new "revenge weapons". Just at the point when victory seemed in sight, it looked as if Britain would buckle under the crushing onslaught of 10,000 V1 flying bombs and 1,400 V2 rockets, launched on England between June 1944 and March 1945. Dispensing with the need for pilots, the V1 could fly a distance of 200 miles and carried one ton of high explosives. The RAF named them "doodlebugs". They also became known as PACs (pilotless aircraft) or buzz bombs as they emitted a portentous buzzing sound that stopped when they were about to drop. For years Hitler had threatened Britain with his "secret weapon". The first V1 was launched over London on 13th June 1944, to avenge the successful Allied landing in Europe the previous week. Unrelentingly until October, V1s continued bombing at a rate of about 50 a week, in total, killing 9,000 civilians and seriously injuring approximately 25,000 others. Britons lived in fear of the ominous silence when a doodlebug's engine stopped, because no one could estimate where it would fall. They either dropped directly or were carried along by the wind. Mirrie Hull recalled: "It was the silence when the engine cut out that was worrying. Then you'd hear a big bang and know you were safe – it had landed somewhere else." After 79 days, the V1 threat was stopped when Allied Forces overran the areas where they were being built.

Then Hitler launched the V2, the world's first rocket, which could fly even further distances than the V1 and travelled at greater speeds. Like the V1, it also carried one ton of high explosives. On 8th September 1944, the Germans launched their first V2s on London from a suburb of The Hague in Holland. Firing at a rate of between four and seven a day, the V2s were not as accurate as Hitler had hoped and they were exceptionally costly. After seven months, V2 rockets had killed 2,754 and injured 6,500.

Lights up

Despite the bombing on some towns and particularly on London, the end of the war was imminent. It was realised that not everywhere would be attacked by the flying bombs and on 17th September 1944, the "dim-out" was introduced to many towns. This was just slightly less stringent than the blackout with a modified form of street lighting allowed. Major cities and coastal towns remained in total blackout and complete blackouts would be imposed anywhere an air raid might take place. Full lifting of the blackout across Britain did not occur until 30th April 1945, one week before the end of the war was announced, when rumours of Hitler's suicide were rife. The blackout had been one of the most resented restrictions of the period and many remember the excitement of seeing their first neon sign and of the brightness of night time streets after so long in darkness. In September 1944, the *Daily Mirror* reported the government's plans for releasing those serving in the armed forces, stating that married women would be treated as a priority class, while other men and women would either be demobbed or would be signed up to work on reconstruction, or rebuilding the country.

Over the next week the announcement that war had ended was eagerly anticipated. On the evening of 7th May, when reports spread that Germany had surrendered, an announcement was made on the radio that the next day would be declared Victory in Europe (VE)

Day and that the Prime Minister would speak to the nation. At 3pm the following day, from the Cabinet room at Number 10, Downing Street, Churchill's speech was broadcast on the radio and relayed over loudspeakers to waiting crowds in Trafalgar Square and Parliament Square. He proclaimed that the war was over and there would be two days' national holiday to celebrate. He paid tribute to the men and women who had laid down their lives and to all those who had fought valiantly on land, sea and in the air. Euphoric crowds surged through the streets, shouting, singing and cheering. Soon after the broadcast, thousands gathered outside Whitehall and chanted for Churchill. Eventually he appeared on the balcony of the Ministry of Health building and began an impromptu speech:

> "This is your victory. It is the victory of the cause of freedom in every land. In all our long history, we have never seen a greater day than this. Everyone, man or woman, has done their best. Everyone has tried...God bless you all."

Huge crowds also gathered on the Mall outside Buckingham Palace and cheered as the King, Queen and their daughters the Princesses Elizabeth and Margaret, appeared on the palace balcony. Later that day, the Prime Minister appeared with them on the balcony and for the first time in nearly six years, all the blackout curtains had been taken down and every room in the palace glittered with light. Later the King spoke to the waiting nation, thanking "Almighty God for a great deliverance" and declaring that throughout the conflict, the people were "never for one moment daunted or dismayed." He continued by acknowledging all who had fought so bravely, urging everyone to: "...resolve as a people to do nothing unworthy of those who died for us and to make the world such a world as they would have desired, for their children and for ours."

Celebrations
For a short time all over Britain, everyone forgot their cares and celebrated. The enormous task of getting the country back to normal was pushed aside. Church bells rang out across the country and churches were packed as people went to offer thanks and to reflect

on the millions of lives lost and hardship endured. Mayors and other dignitaries followed Churchill's broadcast with local speeches. Housewives and others who had struggled to maintain morale for the last few years organised celebratory parties, once again calling upon their creativity and enterprising spirits, as they fashioned bunting, rosettes, flags and fancy dress costumes out of odds and ends, raiding their sewing boxes and larders and improvising party food from their rations to share with their families and neighbours. Neighbours pooled ration coupons, children helped by making paper flags, party hats and costumes, and many bought crepe paper bunting, rosettes and red, white and blue flags from shops that had been beginning to stockpile such things for weeks. Bunting was strung across streets, tables and chairs pushed together and covered with tablecloths and across the country, everyone rejoiced. Proportionate to the inventive spirits of the last few years, tales of the children's fancy dress costumes were startlingly enterprising and original, despite the dearth of materials. Extremely inventive mothers, grandmothers and aunties used whatever materials they could find, such as blackout curtains, adults' clothes, sheets and pillowcases and even Christmas decorations to quickly make costumes representing topical, historical and fictional figures, including "Freedom", "Britannia", "Rationing", "Red Tape", "Victory", munitions workers, brides and countless nurses and Winston Churchills. Bonfires were lit, many in the centres of roads and many accompanied by fireworks. Eyewitnesses report that the food and drink for those celebrations was astonishing and little short of miraculous considering the rationing that was still in place. The celebrations continued for several days. There was so much to rejoice about: the war in Europe was over; Britain and its allies had won; evacuees and some troops would soon be returning home; air raids and flying bombs were consigned to memories.

"Let us not forget the toil and efforts that lie ahead"
When Churchill made his radio broadcast on 8th May, he had also said:

> "We may allow ourselves a brief period of rejoicing, but let us not forget for a moment the toil and efforts that lie ahead."

The toil and efforts were indeed going to be enormous. Half a million homes had been destroyed, thousands more severely damaged; thousands of civilians had been killed and millions of lives disrupted. Many – particularly children and the elderly – experienced nightmares and nervous problems for years to come; most mourned loved ones and the realisation that austerity was to continue was difficult to bear. By 15th August, when Victory in Japan was declared, World War Two was truly, finally over. A victory parade had been held in London on 10th August, when once again huge crowds of cheering, flag-waving crowds took to the streets, but compared to VE Day, VJ Day was more subdued. Although the troops abroad rejoiced as they would be returning home, conscription would continue until 1963 and many returned to damaged or obliterated homes. Britain desperately needed money to pay for reconstruction and also to import food for a country that continued to suffer severe shortages. Women who had worked in "proper" jobs for the first time in their lives and gained independence and a sense of self-worth through it, would have to give up those jobs and return to pre-war passivity when the men returned. For many, after the initial jubilation came a feeling of deflation. Jackie Watson commented: "In some ways, after the end of the war it was worse because we had won, but there was still rationing for years, which felt so harsh. After the initial euphoria, everything went flat – we were still struggling and under harsh restrictions."

The disenchantment continued. In 1938 there had been 10,000 divorces in Britain, but in 1945 there were 25,000 as people tried to return to the family life they had before the war or the expectations they had hoped for during the war. But everyone had changed. The anxieties, suffering and long separations had taken their toll, many had learned to live independently from their spouses, experiencing enormous events separately, and the strain was just too much for many. It was a case of adjusting to a new normality, but it was almost unrecognisable from the time before the war.

Rationing actually worsened at some points after the war. When the Labour government was elected to power, America stopped sending supplies of powdered egg, Spam and sausage meat. In 1946 bread was rationed for the first time and remained rationed for two years, which at the time was seen as the height of austerity. Those who still had homes had to carry on living with their shabby furnishings and depleted wardrobes for some time, while gardens and parks remained churned up for growing vegetables. Rationing of clothing, fabric and knitting wool that had started in June 1941 continued until 1949. The basic petrol rationing was restored, but it continued to be rationed until 1950, while food rationing continued until 1954.

Restructuring the country

The war had brought out the best in the British people. They had responded to the challenges with fortitude, adaptability and resolve, generating a shared sense of solidarity that continued in the aftermath of the war. In the first few years, resourcefulness and endeavour were needed almost as much as they had been during the conflict. After the surprise landslide result against Churchill's Conservative government in the General Election of 1945, Clement Attlee's Labour government struggled to deal with the problems caused by the war. The Labour Party had promised to rebuild the country with the campaign message "Let us face the future", but it was an enormous task. Living standards had to be improved, the armed forces had to be maintained to face the new threat from Communist Russia, food and other essential goods had to be eked out, the medical profession needed organising to meet the overwhelming post-war demand and the idea of "cradle-to-grave" social security was aimed for.

Health

The threat of German bombing of civilians compelled the government to reorganise hospital services in London in February 1939, seven months before the war started. The Emergency Medical Service (EMS) was established, ensuring that London hospitals and medical staff were ready to care for anyone injured by enemy action and to arrange for patients' treatment in whichever hospital was nearest and available to them. In spite of the enormous number of casualties however, the EMS was never placed under the stress that had been expected. Yet the organisation of the EMS became part of the basis of the National Health Service after the war. At the end of 1942, the economist and social reformer William Beveridge had published a paper: *Social Insurance and Allied Services,* which became known as the Beveridge Report. Based on social surveys that had been carried out between 1918 and 1939, the report provided a summary of principles that Beveridge believed were necessary to eliminate poverty from Britain. He frequently repeated the phrase "abolition of want", arguing for social progression and proposing a system of social security to be operated by the government after the war. He stated: "Want is one only of five giants on the road of reconstruction and in some ways the easiest to attack. The others are Disease, Ignorance, Squalor and Idleness." After the war Aneurin (Nye) Bevan was appointed Minister of Health with the task of tackling the country's severe housing shortage. In 1948, Bevan instituted the National Health Service as well; a free service that was paid for directly through public taxes. The NHS aspired to give everyone equal medical attention and to blur class boundaries. Initially, most doctors were opposed to the NHS, believing that they would lose money through it, but eventually, 95 per cent of all of the medical profession joined. Despite its great ambitions, from its earliest days the NHS was short of money. For instance, Attlee's government had estimated that it would cost £140 million a year by 1950. In actuality, it was costing £358 million by 1950. But it remained a remarkable achievement for all those who had not been able to afford healthcare.

Education

Education was another area desperately in need of reform. Before and during the war, the minimum school leaving age was 14 and costly university fees meant that higher education was only experienced by the rich, but the Education Act of 1944 steered through Parliament by Richard Austen Butler, meant that a good education became more accessible for all after 1945. The Education Act provided free secondary education for all pupils and the school leaving age was raised to 15, though the intention that it should be 16 was not realised until 1972.

Housing

The desperate housing shortage called for desperate measures. After the war over four million council houses and high-rise apartment blocks were built across the country and by the mid-1950s; nearly three million people were re-housed in these estates. Meanwhile, more than 156,000 prefabricated homes were built between 1945 and 1948 as a temporary measure, although many remained for decades. Prefabs were single-storey houses, with no staircases, cellars or lofts. Each had two bedrooms, a living room and a kitchen and bathroom at the back. Most people who moved into them loved these secure, convenient, little detached bungalows. In 1946 the New Towns Act was introduced to deal with the problem of overcrowded city centres and slums. Over the next 20 years several new towns were planned and built, containing all facilities needed by a community. After 1945 higher wages and easier to obtain mortgages meant that more people began buying their own homes

Culture and clothing

In June 1945 the Chancellor of the Exchequer announced that the Council for the Encouragement of Music and the Arts, the CEMA, would continue as a permanent organisation, but would be called The Arts Council of Great Britain. This happened in spring 1946. The policy of the new Council was to remain as it had been with the CEMA: "to encourage the best British national arts, everywhere, and to do it as far as possible by supporting others rather than by setting up state-run monopolies." The government-funded body sought to promote the performing, visual and literary arts to spread the best of culture even further than the CEMA had done so successfully during the war, enabling public money to be used to support the arts and culture across Britain. Also in 1946 the BSI, or British Standards Institute, which set emergency standards during the war to assist uniform and utility clothing production, brought together manufacturers, wholesalers and retailers to resolve the general disorder that occurred with clothes sizing. The fashion trade agreed on one system of sizes for both women's outerwear and children's clothing, which was subsequently replaced by a standard for size marking across all clothes, enabling all manufacturers to cater for different figure shapes and for shoppers to be able to purchase readymade clothes more easily.

The invisible chain

In 1941 George Orwell wrote an essay entitled *England your England*, describing the patriotism of the war as an "invisible chain" that bound Britain together through a sense of comradeship that transcended class boundaries. In spite of everyone's hardships and anxieties, the collective morale and commitment to the war effort remained firm throughout the war years and even beyond, in a spirit of stoical endurance and good humour. Although this morale fluctuated through particularly difficult periods, in general, everyone faced the state of emergency with ingenuity, pride and determination, regardless of their ages, backgrounds, capabilities or beliefs, maintaining a team spirit and inventing new solutions for a wide range of problems.

Women in particular learned a lot from rationing and the invisible chain that supported them throughout the war. Margaret Arthur affirmed: "I learnt to sew and knit, and to cook with limited supplies. Even though I was a child in the war, the whole rationing experience made me appreciate things a lot more and the habit of making do and mending has remained with me for life." Mirrie Hull said: "Everybody helped each other. If a neighbour ran out of something, we all shared what we had even when we were so constrained with rationing. We just made the most of it." The majority of those who grew up in the war years continue to salvage and use whatever they can rather than simply discard things and most are exceptionally careful with all resources. This enterprising, supportive attitude that emerged as the legendary wartime or Blitz spirit was mentioned by everyone who shared their memories for this book. Eric Brown summed it up when he said: "It was a terrible time for sure, but I will never forget the sense of comradeship and companionship, shared by everyone who went through it."

BIBLIOGRAPHY

Books

Bédoyère, Guy de la, *The Home Front*, Shire Books, 2005

Brown, Mike, *A Child's War*, Sutton Publishing Ltd, 2000

Brown, Mike, *Wartime Britain*, Shire Books, 2011

Brown, Mike and Harris, Carol, *The Wartime House*, The History Press, 2001

Chase, Joanna, *Sew and Save*, Literary Press, 1941

Cooksley, Peter G., *The Home Front, Civilian Life in World War Two*, Tempus, 2007

Craig, Elizabeth, *Cooking in Wartime*, Literary Press, 1940

Eating For Victory: Healthy Home Front Cooking on War Rations, Michael O'Mara, 2007

Evans, Paul and Doyle, Christopher, *The 1940s Home*, Shire Books, 2011

Food Facts for the Kitchen Front, Collins, 1941

Good Housekeeping, the Best of the 1940s, Anova, 2008

Goodall, Felicity, *The People's War*, Readers Digest, 2010

Harris, Carol, Women at War 1939-1945, The History Press, 2000

Horth, Lillie B. and Arthur C., *101 Things to do in Wartime*, Batsford, (originally 1940)

Hylton, Stuart, *Careless Talk: The Hidden History of the Home Front*, The History Press, 2003

Hylton, S., *Their Darkest Hour*, Sutton Publishing, 2000

Knitting for All, Odhams Press, 1941

Longmate, N., *How We Lived Then: A History of Everyday Life during the Second World War*, Arrow Books, 1973

Make Do and Mend, Ministry of Information, 1943

Maloney, Alison, *The Forties Good Times Just Around the Corner*, Michael O'Mara, 2005

Middleton, C. H., *Digging for Victory: Wartime Gardening with Mr Middleton*, Aurum Press Ltd, 2008

Middleton, C. H., *Your Garden in Wartime*, Aurum Press Ltd, 2010

Patten, Marguerite, *We'll Eat Again*, Hamlyn, 1985

Patten, Marguerite, *Victory Cookbook: Nostalgic Food and Facts from 1940-1954*, Bounty Books, 2002
The British Home Front Pocket Book, Ministry of Information, 1940-42
The Home Workshop, Odhams Press, c.1945

Leaflets
Civil Defence Leaflets
Dig for Victory Leaflets
Grow More Food, 1939
Potato Pete's Recipe Book, 1945

Places to visit
Bletchley Park, The Mansion, Bletchley Park, Milton Keynes, MK3 6EB. Website: www.bletchleypark.org.uk Telephone: 01908 640404
Chartwell, Mapleton Road, Westerham, TN16 1PS. Website: www.nationaltrust.org.uk/chartwell Telephone: 01732 868381
Chislehurst Caves, Old Hill, Chislehurst, Kent, BR7 5NL. Website: www.chislehurstcaves.co.uk Telephone: 020 8467 3264
Churchill War Rooms, Clive Steps, King Charles Street, London SW1A 2AQ. Website: cwr.iwm.org.uk Telephone: 020 7930 6961
Clifford Road Air Raid Shelter, Clifford Road Primary School, Clifford Road, Ipswich, Suffolk IP4 1PJ. Website: www.cliffordroadshelter.org.uk
Eden Camp Modern History Theme Museum, Malton, North Yorkshire, YO17 6RT. Website: http://www.edencamp.co.uk Telephone: 01653 697777
Geffrye Museum Trust, 136 Kingsland Road, London, E2 8EA. Website: www.geffrye-museum.org.uk Telephone: 020 7739 9893
Home Front Experience, New Street, Llandudno LL30 2YE. Website: www.homefrontmuseum.co.uk Telephone: 01492 871032
Imperial War Museum, Lambeth Road, London SE1 6HZ. Website: www.iwm.org.uk Telephone: 020 7416 5000
Imperial War Museum North, The Quays, Trafford Wharf Road, Manchester M17 1TZ. Website: www.iwm.org.uk Telephone: 0160 836 4000
Stockport Air Raid Shelters, 61 Chestergate, Stockport, Cheshire SK1 1NE. Website: www.stockport.gov.uk/airraidshelters Telephone: 0161 474 1940
Winston Churchill's Britain at War Experience, 64-66 Tooley Street, London Bridge, London SE1 2TF. Website: www.britainatwar.co.uk Telephone: 020 7403 3171

ACKNOWLEDGEMENTS

I would like to thank everyone who shared their stories of the war with me. So many people, so many memories! Thank you in particular to Stan Bell, Yvonne Gilan, Mirrie Hull, Anne Maltby, John Maltby and Jackie Watson, who spent time patiently relating their fascinating experiences.

This book is dedicated to Maisie Walker who was an incredible source of information and shared so much with me, never tiring of answering my questions. She epitomises the positive British spirit! I would also like to dedicate it to the memory of my mum Jean, and my grandmother Kitty, who told me their stories as I grew up and ultimately inspired me to write the book in the first place.

INDEX